STRATEGIES
OF THE GREAT
FOOTBALL COACHES

STRATEGIES
OF THE
GREAT FOOTBALL COACHES

BY HANK NUWER

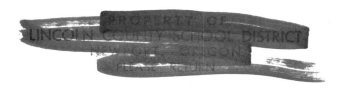

Franklin Watts
New York/London/Toronto/Sydney/1988

Photographs courtesy of:
Hank Nuwer: pp. 20, 41, 61 (OU Sports Information),
121, 129;
UPI/Bettmann Newsphotos: pp. 27, 46, 71, 80, 91, 98,
108.

Diagrams by Vantage Art, Inc.

Library of Congress Cataloging-in-Publication Data
Nuwer, Hank.
Strategies of the great football coaches / by Hank Nuwer.
p. cm.
Bibliography: p.
Includes index.
Summary: Discusses the careers of coaches whose innovative
strategy changed the game of football, including John William
Heisman, Knute Rockne, Vince Lombardi, Bear Bryant, Tom
Landry, and others.
ISBN 0-531-10518-0
1. Football—United States—Coaches—Biography—Juvenile
literature. [1. Football—Coaches.] I. Title.
GV939.A1N88   1988
796.332'092'2—dc19
[B]
[920]   87-25434   CIP   AC

CONTENTS

STRATEGIES OF THE GREAT FOOTBALL COACHES

PREFACE
THE FIELD GENERALS OF FOOTBALL

Ever since the game of football was first played in its modern form, on November 6, 1869 (Rutgers vs. Princeton), fans have speculated on the strategies and winning ways of America's best coaches. Over the years many coaches have walked onto the gridiron, but only a relatively few have become legends. The game's demands upon coaches have themselves become a part of American folklore. Weaker men have cracked under the strain. Football coaches have quit under fire, emotionally broken down, and even committed suicide.

But this book intends to honor those coaches who not only gained fame as winners, but who also won reputations as field generals in a tactical sense. In short, the innovations and refinements they made in the game are celebrated here as well as their lives. The great coaches were, and are, those men who knew how to manage both information and talent.

Readers will be introduced to a dozen of the most prominent coaches, both past and present, with emphasis on the strategies used by these coaches. All the coaches included in this book considerably influenced the sport. To be in this book, each man also had to have coached for at least ten years, preferably with the same team for most of his career.

Because pro football has enjoyed phenomenal attention for a shorter time than has college football, which gained wide popularity in the mid-fifties, there have been fewer noteworthy innovators in the pro ranks than there have been in the colleges. The men selected for this book were selected not only on the basis of wins and percentage of wins, but also on the length of the shadows they cast during their careers.

Among college coaches, only those who spent the bulk of their careers with a *major* university were included, eliminating otherwise notable coaches such as Grambling's Eddie Robinson, whose many victories were gained against lesser competition. The quality-of-competition factor also eliminated Brigham Young University's LaVell Edwards. Another criterion for selecting coaches was their performance in post-season games: major bowls for college coaches or the championship game/Super Bowl for professional coaches. For example, because of their teams' poor performance in post-season play, Michigan's Bo Schembechler and Tennessee's Bob Neyland were not included in this book. Also, only the best coach from a particular college or for a professional team has been included; for that reason, Knute Rockne was chosen over the great Frank Leahy to represent Notre Dame. Finally, an effort has been made to represent all eras of football, from its rather shaky beginnings to its stronghold in American culture today.

It is the author's hope that this book will help the reader see these great coaches as flesh-and-blood men. They were the greatest in their profession, but they still possessed human flaws and frailties.

1

AMOS ALONZO STAGG: THE OLD PIONEER

Football was first played in America, albeit in a primitive form, by the Puritans during the early 1600s. The game involved nothing more complicated than kicking an inflated pig's bladder toward an opponent's goal, while your opponent used whatever force he deemed necessary to prevent you from scoring. So dangerous was the sport considered back then that the town of Boston passed a law calling for a fine of twenty shillings for participating in the game.

Over the next 250 years, the game stagnated. Football contests were bloody events, settled with fists, not with finesse. So much did the sport endanger the health of participants that Harvard and Yale abolished it in 1860. By coincidence, the first football team in the United States that adopted rules intended to civilize the game—the Oneida [N.Y.] Football Club—was organized in 1862, the year that Amos Alonzo "Lonnie" Stagg was born.

The son of a West Orange, New Jersey, farmhand, Amos Alonzo Stagg believed in honesty and clean living. Not only did he not drink, smoke, or use profanity, he felt uncomfortable being with anyone who practiced these vices.

Stagg held that playing well matters more than whether you win or lose. "Live in a way that makes you feel good, and get your fun out of feeling good" was his motto. He lost several games because he refused to bend or break a rule simply to add another win to his record. For example, while coaching at the University of Chicago, he saw his team floundering on the one-yard line but staunchly resisted a temptation to send in a fresh player off the bench with a new play, because, he explained, "the rules committee deprecates the use of a substitute to convey information."

Nonetheless, his cumulative coaching record was impressive. With 314 victories, he not only was the winningest all-time coach in history until Bear Bryant and Eddie Robinson surpassed him, but he also pioneered many aspects of the game that are now taken for granted. In addition, his gentle demeanor and clean lifestyle helped to gradually improve football's image as something more than just a game for rowdies to enjoy.

As a boy, Stagg was so poor that the only footballs he owned were pig bladders that his father gave him at hog-butchering time. He inflated them by inserting a feather quill into the bladder and blowing into the quill, using these "pigskins" to play football with his school chums.

With his fine mind, young "Lonnie" naturally wanted to attend college, even though the odds were against him. To earn enough money to attend Orange High School and, later, prestigious Phillips Exeter Academy for a year ·(to qualify for Yale's rigorous admission requirements), he pitched hay, cut wood, and performed other odd jobs. At Exeter, he subsisted on crackers and milk until he found work there as well. But even with so much time spent trying to earn money, he still managed not only to excel in his studies but also to pitch for the school's baseball team, becoming famous for his curveball and ending up as the squad's captain. However, his life's direction began to change one day when he attended a football match in which Yale vanquished Princeton 6–0. This new sport intrigued young Lonnie. The sight of all those sturdy, muscular players convinced him that he ought to build up his 5-6, 147-pound frame with physical exercise.[1]

Entering Yale's divinity program at twenty-two with $32 in savings that was soon spent on tuition and a down payment on a room, he once again lived on crackers and milk until his body broke down. Fortunately, a kindly school doctor intervened, and Lonnie found work in the student dining room in exchange for his meals, quickly regaining his lost strength and weight.

A chance dare by an acquaintance of Stagg's caused him to try out for Yale's football team which, coincidentally that same year, had purchased its first field. Although he was inexperienced, young Lonnie's natural ability won him a starting position.

Stagg left his divinity school manners at home while playing football. He soon learned to stiff-arm opponents so powerfully that a local newspaper ran a cartoon displaying "Stagg's Ministerial Uppercut."

But Stagg's loyalties were divided between two sports at this time. In 1889, he also pitched for Yale's famed baseball nine and received a $3,000 offer to play professional ball with the New York Nationals. "The whole tone of the game was smelly," he said later, explaining that he turned down the offer because gamblers and alcoholics frequented major league baseball parks.

Following his graduation from Yale, he remained in New Haven to continue his graduate studies, playing both baseball and football. In those days, you could play college ball indefinitely. (Stiff eligibility rules were finally written to prevent this.) In addition to starring on the gridiron, the older, more mature Stagg became an assistant coach to the then head football coach Walter Camp. One of his duties was to serve as a model to teach the other players how to tackle. Coming home bruised and sore every day from practice, Stagg one day had an inspiration. He rolled up a mattress, secured it with ropes, and came up with what he called a "dummy" for players to tackle. His invention, modified considerably, of course, is still used today.

But Stagg also impressed observers on the football field with his talents as an end. In 1889, he was selected to the first All-American football eleven by his coach, Walter Camp.[2]

Ironically, all the while that Stagg starred in athletics at Yale, he was having a serious problem in Divinity School. His grades in classes taught by professors such as William Rainey Harper were acceptable, but Stagg stammered horribly whenever called upon to preach. Slowly it dawned upon him that his difficulties with public speaking meant that a career as a minister was out of the question. Therefore, in 1890, he quit Yale to enroll at the newly founded International YMCA College in Springfield, Massachusetts, and studied to become a coach—an occupation that was to engage him for the next fifty-six years.

Stagg claimed that no team made him prouder than his first Springfield eleven of 1890, particularly since the entire student body was made up of only forty-two students. The freshman coach quickly found that his calculated strategies were enough to foil heavily favored opponents. With enthusiasm and creativity, he invented new plays that before long were a standard part of each coach's playbook.

His first successful play was to improve upon the "wedge" formation used by his old Yale coach, Camp, which consisted of a quarterback handing off to a back, then pushing the man in the back to help his momentum. Stagg's brainstorm was to use the quarterback as Camp always did but to send four men ahead of the carrier to batter the line, opening up holes that frequently led to long gains straight up the middle.

Another idea of Stagg's, a refinement of a suggestion one of his players made, was what he called his "dead man play." The play was one of the first uses of a decoy. Essentially, the quarterback began to sweep right or left, but instead of keeping possession, he handed off to the fullback, who concealed the ball and fell to the ground as if injured. When the opposing team went for the quarterback, who continued to fake a sweep, the fullback sprang into action. Springfield sprung this hidden-ball trick on Harvard's own 5-yard line, resulting in an easy touchdown and the loss of not a few Crimson tempers. One New York writer, according to Stagg biographer Ellis Lucia, called the coach "without doubt the finest football strategist in the United States."[3]

While at the YMCA college, Stagg participated in events that were then quite revolutionary. He coached the team against his alma mater in the first football game ever played under a roof, a 16–10 loss to Yale played at midnight under carbon lights at Madison Square Garden. He also assisted James A. Naismith with a scheme to develop a new indoor game that could be played on a small court. Naismith and Stagg attached half-bushel vegetable baskets to the bottom of the gymnasium's running track. Stagg wrote his sister in Pittsburgh that he thought this new game might have possibilities as a winter sport—a sport that naturally enough came to be called basketball.

The coach thought he might be content to spend the rest of his life in Springfield, but one day his old Bible teacher, Dr. Harper, contacted him with a proposition. Over a pancake breakfast Harper explained that he had recently been named president of a new Chicago-based university to be funded by John D. Rockefeller, and he wanted Stagg to coach and head the physical education department for $1,500 a year.

Stagg, so the legend goes, was struck dumb by this proposition and could think of nothing to say. Dr. Harper misread his old pupil's silence.

"Two thousand dollars and an assistant professorship," said the president.

The coach continued to stare straight ahead, mulling over this turn of events.

"Then I'll give you $2,500 and an associate professorship, which means an appointment for life," he said.

Stagg told Dr. Harper that he wanted some time to consider the offer. He took several weeks to think and pray before writing to say that he would accept. The twenty-nine-year-old coach came to the newly named University of Chicago in 1892, and he stayed forty-one years, until reaching seventy, the age of mandatory retirement, in 1932. Only thirteen players suited up at the first practice, and Stagg was forced to activate himself—again a practice not uncommon during the nineteenth century.

Stagg's arrival at this coeducational institution benefited his life in a personal as well as professional way. He wrote a book entitled *Football* with co-author H. L. Williams, marking the first time that coaching strategies had been discussed in print. Plays were written up in great technical detail as the following certainly illustrates:[4]

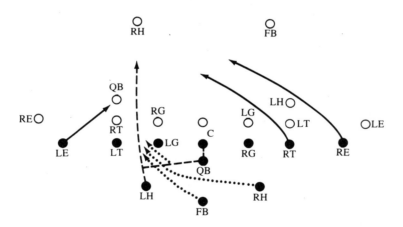

Of greater importance, he courted a seventeen-year-old coed named Stella Robertson soon after arriving in Chicago. The two wed in 1894, and the union lasted sixty-nine years, until the death of the lovely, trim woman Stagg liked to refer to as his first assistant coach. Indeed, for decades she showed up quietly on the sidelines during his practices, scribbling notes into her notebook from time to time. For their honeymoon, the coach took her to California by rail with his Chicago Maroons in December of 1894 to beat Stanford 24–4 in the first ever cross-country game. The "highlight" of the trip was a fire that broke out in the team's shabby Pullman car that the players valiantly extinguished. Had the blaze gotten out of control, they would have had to jump from the car into the freezing, chest-high snows of the Sierra mountains.

While in Chicago, Stagg continued churning out new strategies and adventures. He pioneered the concept of having his quarterback stand over the center to receive the snap. He was first to develop the backfield-in-motion play. He conceived the idea of the option pass play, where the runner chooses to throw or keep the ball, depending upon the reactions of the defense.

On offense, he explored the possibility of using an unbalanced line, moving an offensive lineman to one side of center or the other, thereby creating a "strong" side and "weak" side. He attempted the first onside kick and the first fake kick, originated the Statue of Liberty play, and perfected the reverse, the lateral, the handoff, and other razzle-dazzle plays that infuriated his opponents. Defensively, he created such innovations as the 7–2–2, the 6–2–1–2, and the 5–2–1–2–1 formations.

Stagg's book, *Football*, revealed some of his winning strategies. "Try to make a touchdown during the first two minutes of the game, before the opponents have become fairly waked up," he wrote. "Play a fast game," he advised. "Let one play come after the next in rapid succession without any waits or delays. The more rapidly you play, the more effective it will be. Therefore *line up quickly* and get back in your regular place instantly after making a run."

Stagg, who also invented the playbook, was always

quick to take advantage of rule changes. When the forward pass became legal to throw in 1906, the coach quickly came up with sixty-four pass plays.

Although he won 314 games during his career, Stagg always emphasized that football was only a game, not real warfare. Any player who smoked or cursed was benched on the spot. Stagg never cursed his players to get them to perform their best, not even during an agonizing losing streak in the early 1900s, when President Harper only half-jokingly suggested that the Maroons might do better if they heard an oath now and then.

But Stagg had his ways of goading players. Anyone who made a mental mistake was summarily tossed into the coach's "Jackass Club," and repeat offenders were known as double or triple jackasses.

The players, however, were loyal to Stagg, affectionately calling him the "Old Man" as early as 1899, when Chicago won the first of seven conference championships with a 16–0–2 season. He, in turn, honored those players who combined athletic prowess with sportsmanship, starting the "Order of the C" at Chicago, the forerunner of all lettermen clubs. On special occasions, he invited players over to his house to chat in front of a fireplace while his "first assistant coach" served milk and fresh-baked loaves of bread.

Stagg's days at Chicago were mainly happy, until he reached his seventieth birthday and was drummed out by then-President Robert Maynard Hutchins. The coach reminded Hutchins of his cumulative 268–141 won-lost record, his five undefeated teams, and one national championship, but Hutchins was adamant. The president's action caused a near riot on campus that Stagg himself was called in to quell, and his supporters from across the country

Amos Alonzo Stagg

condemned Hutchins for violating the promise of lifelong employment that President Harper had given Stagg. Shaken by this display of public sentiment, the president tried to cover up by offering Stagg an important-sounding title, but Stagg saw through this charade. "I'm too young to quit," snapped the Grand Old Man.

Stagg's spirits were restored when the job offers in coaching and other fields began to pile up on his desk. He accepted an offer from the College of the Pacific in Stockton, California. Demonstrating very quickly that he possessed the vitality of a man thirty years his junior, in just three years he and Pacific went undefeated to win the Far Western Conference title.

Even in his eighties, Stagg was a strategic genius, claimed Eddie LeBaron, tailback of the 1946 Pacific team and later an NFL quarterback. In an interview with Paul Zimmerman of *Sports Illustrated*, LeBaron said:

"I was the tailback in a spread single-wing. I ran and passed. We'd throw 25 to 26 passes a game. A lot of times our formation was like a shotgun, a lot of motion and movement. Stagg would call his formation Pea Digger Left and Pea Digger Right. He had one formation where he'd set two wide receivers on one side, with one guy behind the other, and we'd throw a screen pass to the back guy—like Washington did in the '83 Super Bowl [against Miami]. He had a pass offense where anyone could throw.

"What he really knew was the kicking game. He'd been the first one to put in the spread punt formation. He'd cross the inside men on punt coverage. People averaged one to two yards on returns against us. I punted. He wanted forty to forty-three yards [per punt], no more, no less. He wanted a one-step approach, so the outside rushers couldn't get to me."[5]

Stagg continued to coach at Pacific until he reached his eighty-fourth birthday in 1946, leaving with a won-lost record of 314–199–17, then football's all-time best. But retirement was out of the question for him. He worked as an assistant coach at tiny Susquehanna University in Selinsgrove, Pennsylvania, helping his son, Amos, Jr., who was head coach, until 1953 when Stella's ill health caused him to take a job as a kicking coach at Stockton Junior College—located a short distance from his old home during college days—to be near her sickbed.

The Grand Old Man didn't retire until his ninety-eighth birthday, and then only because his eyesight began to fail him. He passed away at age 102, a few months after the death of his beloved first assistant coach.

2

JOHN WILLIAM HEISMAN: THE MOST FAMOUS NAME IN COLLEGE FOOTBALL

John William Heisman contributed fifty years to the sport of football as a player, administrator, and coach. Although the game seemed to outgrow him in his later years, he still enjoyed an enviable career, with 185 victories against only 70 defeats and 17 ties.

Always dressed on the gridiron in his familiar black jersey and baseball cap, Heisman ran his practices like a dictator. Every new season he greeted his troops with the same terse message. "This is a football," he would inform his men, holding it up as if it were priceless. "A prolate spheroid—that is, an elongated sphere in which the outer leathern casing is drawn tightly over a somewhat smaller rubber tubing."

At this point, Heisman's voice grew low and grim. "Better to have died as a small boy than to fumble this ball."

Heisman himself was very well acquainted with the prolate spheroid. In his youth he once blocked a kick with his face and carried a dented nose to his grave.

He was born in Cleveland, Ohio, in 1869, but his family soon moved to Titusville, Pennsylvania. His father, at first, fiercely opposed John's decision to play football for Titusville High. Later, when his son entered college, the elder Heisman bet hundreds of dollars on John's teams and was his son's most vocal fan when young John was out of earshot.

Because of relaxed eligibility rules in those early years of the game, Heisman played five years of college ball at two different colleges. Despite his meager 158-pound playing weight, he starred as a tackle at Brown University from 1887 to 1889, and then attended law school at the University of Pennsylvania in 1890 and 1891, playing end and center in addition to tackle. In those early days of the game, free substitution wasn't allowed. The only way a player could leave a game was if he was injured.

The football bug hit Heisman hard, and he eventually quit his legal studies to accept a coaching position at Oberlin College in 1892. He stayed there one year before accepting an offer from the University of Akron (then called Buchtel) but chose to return to Oberlin for one more season in 1894.

At Buchtel College, Heisman's most memorable contribution was to co-invent the center snap (Stagg also experimented with it the same year). Until that time, the center had rolled the ball to the quarterback, like an Easter egg across a lawn. But because Buchtel's quarterback, Harry Clark, was a 6 foot-4 inch giant who had trouble bending to snatch up the rolling ball cleanly, Heisman ordered the center to hike the ball through his legs. That innovation, of course, exists to this day.[1]

While he coached at Oberlin, a minor incident occurred that turned out to have a great deal of significance to Heisman. Heisman's team had fought a bloody battle against another team, and the cost of defending against the popular flying wedge of the day had taken its toll. For the wedge, nine or ten men lined up in front of the ball carrier and steamrolled the opposition. Scores were high, but so were the number of injuries and even fatalities. There were so many, in fact, that a few years later, President Theodore Roosevelt seriously considered a nationwide ban on the sport. Heisman hated the wedge, complaining that no finesse was involved.

After this particular bloody affair, Heisman brought his team home by train. At the depot, eleven men lounged outside, drawing stares from passersby, who eyed their torn clothing, bruised eyes, and multiple lacerations. One woman in particular was horrified. She assumed that such injuries could have been caused by nothing less than a train wreck. The woman's comment disturbed Heisman. He grew determined to do all in his power to civilize the game.

Heisman first made a name for himself at Auburn University (then called Alabama Polytechnic Institute), where he coached from 1895 to 1899. He inherited a team that had been 1–3 under his predecessor, F.M. Hall. He immediately inspired his charges to lose their losing ways. It was not long before a local paper extolled Heisman's virtues in print. "The day on which he arrived at Auburn can well be marked as the luckiest in the history of our football team," reported the *Glomerata*. "Mr. Heisman is not only the best coach that the South has ever seen, but he is a perfect gentleman, and we all love him for his worth."[2] In a two-year span, Heisman's Tigers outscored their opponents 205 to 33.

At Auburn, Heisman became something of the town character. As he did much of the rest of his life, he supplemented his meager coaching salary with money he made as an actor. In those days, "acting" consisted basically of standing on stage and projecting your voice loud enough to take the paint off the ceiling. Heisman always considered himself to be on stage. The locker room was no exception. His players sometimes wished they had a translator handy to help them understand what the coach was talking about.

John William Heisman (right)

"Thrust your projections into their cavities," he exhorted his troops. "Grasp them about the knees and deprive them of their means of propulsion. They must come to earth, locomotion being denied them."

Heisman consciously tried to separate himself from his men, believing that the coach should assume the role of dictator. "At times he must be severe, arbitrary, and little short of a czar," he said. Heisman never asked his players to perform—he ordered them to do so. Neither "please" nor "thank you" was part of his vocabulary. He dictated what foods could be served at the training table, outlawed pork and pastry because he considered them fattening, and advised players to shower in cold water to build toughness.

Fortunately, Heisman also believed in the cerebral approach to football. He insisted that football success could be achieved only if one had certain qualities in sufficient percentages. You needed talent (25 percent), intellect (20 percent), speed (20 percent), aggressiveness (20 percent), and strength (15 percent).[3]

Heisman preferred the swift little man over the beefy, slower man every time. He had never forgotten the incident in which a passerby mistook his players for the casualties of a train wreck. He determined to make the game one of skill and beauty, not one of brute force and bone-crushing tactics that other coaches had made it. One of his major contributions was his one-man fight to institute the forward pass as a major strategic attack to replace the barbaric wedge.

Heisman's inspiration to develop the forward pass came from when he attended a college game between the University of Georgia and the University of North Carolina, held in Atlanta's Brisbine Park. What happened was that when the Tarheel punter dropped back to punt, he was nearly smothered by an onrush of Bulldog jerseys. The North Carolinian panicked and threw the ball downfield instead of kicking it, and the ball landed in the arms of an astounded teammate, who raced 70 yards for a touchdown. The confused officials let the play stand, although the rulebook clearly forbade such chicanery. Georgia Bulldog coach Pop Warner screamed at the injustice of it all.

Interestingly, Pop Warner—whose name later became synonymous with a football league for America's young people—failed to see what Heisman saw: a way to use the forward pass to revolutionize the game. Heisman lobbied with his fellow coaches and rulesmakers to change the law, but it was more than a decade before his efforts succeeded, in 1906. The new play was popularly called "Heisman's forward pass," and in the space of a few years, every coach in America had adopted the strategy—even a reluctant Pop Warner.

But even before Heisman became famous for advocating the adoption of the forward pass, he was well known for other ideas that he promoted. He invented the scoreboard to keep track of the score, first downs, and yardage gained. He was the first to instruct the player calling signals to modulate his voice and use an extra long count, hoping to draw overeager defenders offside. Finally, he lobbied to have the game divided into quarters instead of halves.

Perhaps it was the actor in Heisman, but for whatever reason, he loved plays that involved deception. Coaching in an era when it was illegal to call plays from the bench, Heisman nonetheless used his handkerchief to transmit signals to his players.

One day Heisman visited the dormitory room of two Auburn players, Reynolds Tichenor and Walter Shafer, to discuss football strategies. The coach had devised a play he called "the hidden ball," but he had not yet figured the best way to implement it. "You know, boys, I had a kid ask me once if it was against the rules to hide the ball," said Heisman. "I don't see anything against it, but I honestly don't see how you could work a trick like that."

Shafer offered a suggestion. "Tichenor here is the quarterback," he said. "Why not hide it under his jersey?"

"Put a jersey on, Reynolds," commanded Heisman. "Let's see if it works."

All that evening, the trio experimented with ways to hide the ball under Tichenor's shirt. Finally, Heisman was satisfied and departed. A few weeks later, in an important game against Vanderbilt, the coach sprung the play.

Since the center in those days was the only player required to stand on the line, Heisman dropped the guards and tackles back to form almost a circle around the quarterback. Tichenor took the center snap and faked a handoff to a running back. The wall of players around Tichenor allowed him to slip the ball undetected under his shirt. Vanderbilt fell for the sucker play and Tichenor scored. (Unfortunately, the ruse was not enough to assure the Auburn Tigers of a victory. Vanderbilt eked out a 9–6 win.)

Heisman's next stop was at Clemson, where he coached the Tigers from 1900 to 1903. When Heisman first came to the pretty northwest South Carolina college, he was annoyed to find his players wearing shinguards under knee-length socks, which looked much like the protection that today's soccer players wear. One of his first actions was to ban the shinguards, insisting that they hampered his players' mobility. However, perhaps recalling how his own nose had been permanently squashed, he allowed players to wear the noseguards that had become popular in the 1890s.

Heisman was well known for taking advantage of field conditions. In his first game against Furman, the coach was amazed to find that a towering oak grew right on the football field, and he quickly decided to take advantage of the fact. As was his style, he quickly drew up a play that had a Clemson runner race up the sideline while blockers pushed back Furman defenders until the stout tree was between them and the ball carrier.[4]

It was not unusual for Heisman to dream up new plays on the day of the game, and his Tigers followed his directions that day to the letter. The first time Heisman called the play, he rejoiced to see his runner break into the open. Although the player was caught from behind, he managed to get close enough to the goal line so that the ball could be run over in a more conventional manner a few plays later.

Heisman believed in the element of surprise. In 1902, just before the Tigers left for Atlanta to play Georgia Tech, the coach learned that opposing fans planned to spend a small fortune wining and dining the Tigers to make sure the players would be in no condition to play the next day. Sure enough, a huge Atlanta contingent greeted the Tigers and partied with them practically until game time. But Clemson played a practically flawless game, whipping Tech 44–5. Atlantans soon realized that it was they who had been had. Heisman had sent ahead a full load of bench warmers to serve as decoys, while the first team left the train one stop ahead and enjoyed a restful and sober stay in the tiny town of Lula, Georgia.[5]

The following year, Heisman let word out that his star player, Vet Sitton, was injured, and that he feared the game would result in a Georgia Tech rout. But unbeknownst to Tech, Heisman had carefully groomed a flashy runner named Gil Ellison to replace Sitton. The Tigers annihilated their opponents 73–0.

Atlanta opened its collective wallet after the season and offered Heisman a $50 raise to come to Georgia Tech. There the new coach again took a hapless team and converted it into a winner in a short time. Tech at one point won thirty consecutive games, taking the Southern championship every year from 1914 to 1917. The squad beat Cumberland College by a 222–0 score, a record for the most points scored in a college game. (This record will never be equaled now that coaches have an unwritten rule not to cause humiliation by running up a score.) Poor Cumberland never even made a first down in that game.

Heisman continued to come up with innovations that impressed his contemporaries with their originality. He introduced what came to be known as the Heisman shift.

A New York sportswriter once offered this description of the Heisman shift: "The entire team, except the center, dropped behind the scrimmage zone. The four backs took their post in Indian file at right angles to the rush line, forming the letter *T*." The Heisman shift, although unusual and not as popular as the so-called Notre Dame shift, was admired by many coaches and was used for decades. The formation was so balanced that it could attack either side with equal power. And because the rules then required no pause from the offense, the defense frequently was unable to react until it was too late.

Heisman also wrote a book, called *Principles of Football* (1922), that serves as an invaluable source of understanding his coaching strategies. Here are some of Heisman's maxims:

—Try end runs on first or second down. Never order two end runs in succession. Never attempt an end run when the ball is less that 25 yards away from your own goal, unless you do so from punt formation.

—Punt immediately on first down when hemmed in on your own goal line. When in doubt, punt. (This last maxim has become a household expression.)

—If behind in the second half because your running game has stalled, switch to a passing attack.

—Any runner should be able to carry the ball at least three times in succession. However, do not overtax one player.

—Always direct a play at a newly inserted substitute before he has time to "get into" the game.

Heisman left Georgia Tech under unusual circumstances. When he and his wife decided to divorce, Heisman left Atlanta because he did not want to live in the same city as her. The coach did not know it at the time, but he would never again achieve the kind of success he had at Georgia Tech. In his years of decline, he coached at the University of Pennsylvania, Washington and Jefferson, and, finally, the Rice Institute, before accepting a post as athletic director of the Downtown Athletic Club in New York. He died of pneumonia on October 3, 1936, and the Downtown Athletic Club honored him by naming the most coveted individual award in the sport after him—the Heisman Trophy—which goes to the outstanding college player of the year.

3

FIELDING "HURRY-UP" YOST: A DYNASTY TO REMEMBER

Fielding Harris Yost came to Ann Arbor, Michigan, in 1901, burdened by his reputation as a head coach with "happy feet"—a man who was never content to stay very long in the same job. But he found a home at the University of Michigan, and he never left it. With the Wolverines he headed the greatest dynasty in Big Ten football. Yost's remarkable coaching record on his retirement was 196 victories against only 36 defeats and 12 ties, for a winning percentage of .828. During his twenty-five-year dynasty at Michigan, his teams won 165 games, lost only 29, and tied 10.

Yost was a West Virginian by birth, born in 1871 in a log cabin located within walking distance of the Pennsylvania border. His father's name was Permenus and his mother's was Elzena; his own unusual name of Fielding seems less strange by comparison.

The boy was as solid as an oak tree and the last one any of his friends would challenge to a fistfight. By the time he reached his late teens, he already carried nearly two hundred pounds on his herculean frame, earning his spending money as a deputy marshal in the poor mining towns of his native state.

But Yost dreamed of a more genteel existence, and he took another job teaching public school. More than one strapping country boy found that a polished oak board applied vigorously to the posterior region had a measurable effect on intellectual performance. When he had saved enough money, he quit his job and attended Ohio Normal College for two years. His education there completed, Yost worked in the oil fields long enough to save tuition to attend West Virginia Law School. While there, the straight A student played his first game of football at the not-so-tender age of twenty-four and liked it so much that he signed up to play for three teams concurrently, including Lafayette College's. Blessed not only with size but an aggressive nature, Yost played tackle, a bruiser who loved nothing better than knocking down blockers to reach a ball carrier.

Two years after the football bug bit him, he decided that coaching football was the profession for him. He traveled to Columbus, Ohio, to meet with a faculty representative from Ohio State University but ruined his opportunity when he manhandled the professor during a typically exhuberant Yost "discussion" of football fundamentals. The Ohio State representative ordered the "madman" out of his home.[1]

Yost managed to obtain a coaching position at Ohio Wesleyan instead, but his restless nature left him uneasy in such a quiet environment. From 1897 to 1900, he drifted around the country as an itinerant coach, leaving Ohio Wesleyan for one-year stints, respectively, at the University of Nebraska, the University of Kansas, and Stanford. While working at Stanford, he supplemented his income by coaching simultaneously at four other schools: San Jose Teachers College, California Ukiah, and two high schools in San Francisco. He worked from early morning until it was too dark to see the football any longer. However, he was far from wealthy. Only Stanford paid him much of a salary, and when the Pacific Coast Conference barred non-alumni coaches from coaching, he was again minus a job. Word reached him that President Angell at the University of Michigan was looking for a new head coach, so Yost sent him a letter of application that was filled with carefully folded press clippings.

According to Michigan legend, when the thirty-year-old Yost arrived in Ann Arbor in 1901, he amused Athletic Director Charles Baird by flaunting several scrapbooks filled with articles about his playing and coaching career. Told by Baird that only twenty of Michigan's two thousand students traditionally went out for football, Yost insisted he'd make a few changes. "Athletics for all is Michigan's motto now that Yost is here," the newcomer, dressed in a newsboy-style cap and an ill-pressed suit, told Baird. "There are three things that make a winning football team: spirit, manpower, and coaching. If your boys love Michigan, they've got the spirit, you see. If they'll turn out, that takes care of the manpower. I'll take care of the coaching."

Yost liked to talk a lot. It was said that he coached football all day and talked football all night. Famed sportswriter Ring Lardner said he never once talked to Yost. "My father taught me never to interrupt," quipped Lardner.

But Yost knew how to back up his promises. Fearing that Michigan might possess less talented athletes than he was used to coaching, Yost brought three top players to Ann Arbor on the train with him. In his early years, the coach violated several rules about eligibility, but as he grew older, no one played more by the book than he did, and he regretted his past transgressions.

Those handpicked players for Yost's first Wolverine team were Iowan Dan McGugin, destined to marry Yost's sister; Californian George "Dad" Gregory, one of the most famous men to wear Michigan's maize and blue colors; and Oregonian Willie Heston, who scored more than a hundred touchdowns during his four-year career. The three showed up at the first practice to find their coach, wearing a heavy knit sweater and his trademark battered hat, yelling at his team to show more hustle.

"Hurry-up, hurry-up!" he'd shout. "If you can't do it, I'll find the men that can. Hurry, hurry-up!" It didn't take long before the coach earned the nickname of "Hurry-Up" Yost.

Yost's nickname reflected his own football philosophy, and he revolutionized the game by preferring swift, versatile athletes to the hulks that other coaches of the Big Nine (later to be called the Big Ten) favored. Typical of the athletes Yost favored was Heston, destined to become not only an All-American in 1903 and 1904 but also the most famous halfback in the country during his reign at Michigan.

To put himself through school, the sturdy, 185-pound Heston used his strong back to unload coal cars every morning before classes. He had so little money when he came to Ann Arbor that Yost had to buy him a pair of running shoes. No one, not even the Olympic sprinter Archie Hahn, could match him in a 40-yard dash. His powerful legs gave him tremendous acceleration, allowing him to make long gains out of the slightest holes his offensive linemen provided. "Use your searchlights [eyes] and jump the dead ones [blocked opponents on the ground]," said Heston, describing his manner of running.

Thanks to the heroics of Heston, Boss Weeks, Neil Snow, McGugin, and Gregory, Yost's teams from 1901 to 1905 were called the "Point-a-Minute" gang, although the Wolverines did not actually average 70 points a game. (Teams played seventy-minute games until 1906.) Nonetheless, Michigan's scoring record was impressive. For example, the 1902 team averaged 58 points per contest. During those years when a touchdown was worth only 5 points, Michigan scored 2,821 points to the opposition's 42 points, helping the Wolverines amass a 55–1–1 record. In Yost's 1901 rookie season, his offense ran for 8,000 yards and scored 550 points, while his defense gave up not a single point. They smashed the University of Buffalo 128–0, prompting one of the losing Bulls to sit on the Michigan bench during the game's waning moments.

"You're on the wrong side, son," Yost admonished him.

"Oh, no, I ain't," retorted the battered Buffalonian, staying put. "I was before."

At the close of the 1901 season, Stanford—also undefeated that year—invited its former coach to play in a special game to honor the annual Pasadena Rose Festival. The president of the Tournament of Roses Association, James H. Wagner, hoped the so-called "Rose Bowl" game might become an annual affair.

That game revealed Yost's coaching strategies to the eyes of the nation. A firm believer that the best athletes on the field should play both offense and defense, he used only eleven players the entire game, causing the two Wolverine substitutes to jump in a mud puddle after the game to fool people into thinking they had participated in the match.

Michigan opened the game in frustrating fashion, managing to stall three drives near the Stanford Indians' goal line before scoring in the twenty-third minute of play. But before the half ended, Yost's men had earned 17 tallies. The final score was 49–0, giving Michigan its first national championship. The game mercifully was shortened by ten minutes to keep the fatigued Indians from suffering serious injuries. The Wolverines rushed for 1,463 yards, including a 40-yard bootleg by Willie Heston, an innovation of Yost's that is still being used by runners today.

The bootleg formation relied totally on deception. The play received its name from the way the runner hid the ball against his thigh while rolling out. Yost's formation had ten men line up to the right of center. The snap went to the quarterback, who faked a handoff to the fullback, who in turn smashed into the line behind his ten blockers. When the defense bit, the quarterback flipped the ball to Heston, who hid the ball behind his leg on a surprise sweep to the vacant weak side. Yost liked to refer to this play as "Old 83," and although it was ruled illegal in 1931, coaches who later used the split-T formation employed hard-running quarterbacks who could keep or pitch the ball off at the last possible second.

Old 83 was not the first play devised by Yost for the elusive, cagey Heston. The most revolutionary one was the much-copied tailback formation. In this formation Heston stood about 5 yards behind the center to accept a direct snap. Depending on the call and the reactions of the defense, Heston ran either to the left or to the right with the ball. Heston's powerful running literally shredded the traditional 9–2 defense of the day, forcing opponents to go to a seven-man line. The seven-man line became the norm on defense until the development of a sophisticated passing game.

The passing game, incidentally, owed much to the Michigan coach's inventive mind. He was the first coach to state the philosophy that the passing offense was most effective when used in combination with the run, to keep the defense off balance. Nonetheless, Yost did not ignore the defensive aspect of the game. When he had Germany Schulz on his outstanding 1904 defensive line, Yost allowed the All-American to drop back from the line of scrimmage instead of always charging, making the rover as effective as a middle linebacker.

Yost also encouraged his quarterbacks as early as 1907 to throw bullet spirals that reached the receiver with plenty of zip on the ball. Before this, quarterbacks had thrown lob passes that had as much chance of being intercepted or knocked down as they did of being completed. Yost also developed the concept of a shovel pass behind scrimmage; this pass was considered so unorthodox that officials ruled it illegal the first time Michigan used it, in a game against the University of Pennsylvania.

Yost incorporated the forward pass as a potent offensive weapon as early as 1910. Against the favored Gophers of the University of Minnesota, Yost unveiled a picture-perfect pass play in a game he boasted was "the finest I've ever seen."

With time running out, Michigan's quarterback handed the ball to All-American running back Stan Wells, who faked a run, jerked on the brakes, and completed a pass to Stan Borleske who then went out of bounds on the Minnesota 30-yard line. On the very next play, Michigan lined up without a huddle (another Yost trademark) and ordered the same call, taking the Wolverines down to the 3-yard line. Wells made the game-winning touchdown in a 6–0 Michigan upset.

Throughout his career, Yost presented an imposing picture on the sideline, black cigar jammed between his lips and a felt hat carried low on his brow. His motto was that a good offense was the best defense, and he developed teams that were literally scoring machines. "Football games aren't won, they're lost," he liked to say, developing teams that almost never lost the ball on fumbles and that used the punt as a weapon to keep the enemy deep in its own territory—the so-called punt-pass-pray offense.

Yost was the first to use the man-in-motion as a decoy, a play in which a running back scampered parallel to the line of scrimmage in his own backfield before the ball was hiked. As Yost figured it, the man-in-motion gave the enemy defense fits when it keyed on this man, who often never touched the ball. Yost was also one of the first field generals to realize that lateral field position was important because certain plays worked better on one side of the field than another.

And Yost improved with age. The Michigan coach "never knew there was a calendar," Grantland Rice once wrote. During the 1924 season, a fatigued Yost followed his doctor's orders and retired, but when successor George

Fielding Yost

Little failed to perform up to expectations, the old coach reinstated himself.

If Yost had a fault, it was the sin of pride. "Listen to Yost" was his favorite expression, and he loved talking about himself in the third person. He loathed playing second fiddle to anyone. On the banquet circuit, he would fidget nervously while others talked at the podium, content only when all eyes were upon him. Other coaches avoided the press like the plague; he cultivated media contacts and enjoyed pulling out press clippings to show his players what sportswriters had said about him in print. When he grew displeased with the way the Big Ten was conducting business, the surly Yost helped lead a movement to have Michigan secede from the conference, a secession that lasted several seasons. He was also a thrifty man who even insisted that the play-by-play radio announcers of a Michigan-Wisconsin game pay their way into the ballpark.

Yost could also be insufferable after a victory. When his Michiganers held the great Red Grange to 56 yards in twenty-five carries, Yost gloated after the game. "The Ol' Redhead didn't gain enough ground to bury him in," chortled Yost, "not even if they buried him head down."[2]

On occasion the joke was upon Yost. For years he was rankled by the sight of Wisconsin's live mascot, a badger, and wrote hundreds of letters in an attempt to secure a live wolverine to parade around during Michigan games. Finally, ten wolverines from Alaska were shipped to Yost, but these proved so vicious that he was forced to give all but one—a terror named Biff—to various zoos.

Ironically, Yost's most famous team was that first squad of 1901, but he believed his 1925 team was the best he ever coached. Outscoring the opposition 227 points to 3, Michigan lost only one game that season, a 3–2 heartbreaker to Northwestern. That year the Wolverines scraped by Red Grange's Illinois team 3–0, thumped Navy 54–0, bombed Minnesota 35–0, and skinned Indiana 63–0. The passing combination of quarterback Benny Friedman and receiver Bennie Oosterbaan was one of college football's all-time greatest aerial pairings.

Yost never quite grew used to Michigan's ferocious winters. For many years, at the close of a season, he would travel south to practice law and swap football stories with his brother-in-law, Dan McGugin, who had become head coach at Vanderbilt. An expert in military history, he agonized over Custer's defeat his whole life, working out strategies in his head that the general might have used. He also memorized the details of every major campaign of the Civil War and would set up chairs during a conversation to signify Northern and Southern troop formations.

During Yost's brilliant career, Michigan won or tied eleven conference titles. After his retirement from coaching in 1926, Yost became athletic director at Michigan and held the job until 1941. He died of gallbladder disease in 1946.

Today, a grateful, tradition-bound University of Michigan hasn't forgotten Hurry-Up. One is always added to the attendance figures for Wolverine games. This extra one is for Yost's ghost.

4

KNUTE ROCKNE:
THE SAINT OF SOUTH BEND

Knute Rockne dominated football during the 1920s, the aptly named Golden Age of sports, by becoming the first coach to popularize the college game. In thirteen years as head coach of Notre Dame, from 1918 to 1930, he won 105 games, losing only 12 and tying 5, for a phenomenal .881 winning percentage. Rockne never once suffered a losing season. His teams went undefeated for a full season five times, and six won national championships.

Rockne was a Norwegian immigrant who fell in love with the way Americans played football. Only five feet, eight inches tall and rotund as a steamboat's pilot house, he was anything but a matinee idol in appearance, although eventually Hollywood stars such as Rudolph Valentino sought his company. Columnist Westbrook Pegler claimed the coach had the face of a battered oil can, but his appearance suited his tough, hard-driving nature. "Show me a good and gracious loser and I'll show you a failure," Rockne often said.

Early in life, Rockne displayed a flair for attracting attention. Born in Voss, Norway, on March 4, 1888, the boy made headlines in his tiny village at age five by managing to strand himself atop an ice floe that carried him toward the center of a large lake. Only the keen eyes of a villager spared him an icy death. Rescuers climbed into a boat to retrieve the shivering youngster.

A few months later, his father, Lars Rockne, who had found work in Chicago, sent passage money to Norway for his wife Martha, three daughters, and Knute. During the voyage young Knute scampered up a mast into the steamer's crow's nest, because he wanted to be the first to see his adopted land. A few years later, he discovered baseball and by stopping a sizzling smash with his face earned the flattened nose that became his trademark.

Rockne was a natural athlete, excelling in track and field, baseball, and football, even though he was always the smallest boy in the group. Like other sandlot players of that era, he never wore a helmet in the games he played for his fellow "Swedes." His one concession to safety was applying adhesive tape to his ears, to prevent them from being ripped off.

Rockne's obsession with sports nearly cost him an education. He had a deplorable record for absences at North West Division High School, and his grades were mediocre. At his father's urging, he quit school in his junior year to work at the post office.

Fortunately, by age twenty-two, Rockne decided that he could best pursue his first love if he went to college. Because two friends had gained acceptance to a small Indiana college named Notre Dame, he wrote to the school asking permission to take a high school equivalency examination. His decision to attend a Catholic college disturbed his parents, who practiced the Lutheran faith, but they didn't forbid him to do it.

The future coach arrived on the South Bend, Indiana, campus in September 1910, wearing his only suit, a double-breasted style. A picture taken at this time reveals a cocky young man whose sparse hair made him look more like a young instructor than a college freshman. His life's dream was to become a pharmacist and run his own drugstore.

Notre Dame had been founded in 1842 on Lake St. Mary's by a French priest named Father Edward Sorin. Ironically, Father Sorin founded this school that one day

would bear the nickname "The Fighting Irish" because he hoped to educate and to provide religious training for his fellow countrymen who lived in the remote outpost of Indiana. From two pupils who bartered their labor for tuition, the college slowly grew over the years, offering an excellent education in a strict religious setting.

Rockne, the one-time high school truant, really enjoyed his studies, particularly the chemistry classes he took from Father Julius Nieuwland, destined to become the celebrated discoverer of synthetic rubber. Rockne graduated magna cum laude, with honors in chemistry, bacteriology, and biology.

Rockne's soon-to-become famous determination helped him become a football player at Notre Dame. Although he later told tales about his ineptness as a freshman player for football coach Frank "Shorty" Longman, saying he fumbled a punt and performed poorly at fullback, Rockne actually performed quite credibly during the 1910 season. A story in the *South Bend Tribune*, written by Coles Phinzy, said he was "making good at fullback."[1]

Whatever the truth about his freshman year, Rockne certainly excelled in football as an upperclassman. During his sophomore year, he displayed his talents to a new coach, John L. Marks. Rockne not only made the team but started at left end and, two years later, in his senior year, was elected team captain.

During his last season, with the blessing of another Irish coach, Jesse Harper, who arrived in 1913, Rockne and his roommate, quarterback Gus Dorais, decided to take advantage of a new rule easing restrictions on the forward pass. Rockne didn't invent the forward pass, as many claimed, but his success with it forever changed the sport. Where other receivers displayed the mobility of

Knute Rockne

overfed bison, standing stock still until the football smacked into their chests, he perfected the art of relaxing his hands to snag a toss while running at top speed. He also invented the concept of a receiver running pass patterns, adding primitive fakes, cuts, and curls to deceive enemy defenders.

Notre Dame unveiled its secret weapon at West Point on November 1, 1913, against heavily favored Army. Rockne, after faking a leg injury for several plays, grinned at Dorais in the huddle. "Let's show them something," he whispered. On the snap, Rockne brush-blocked a tackle and then lit out for the undefended flat, where he snagged a 25-yard toss from Dorais. It was the first touchdown registered against Army on a forward pass. During the second half, the Irish relied heavily on a passing attack against the bigger, stronger Cadets, with seven completions going to Rockne. Notre Dame trounced Army 35–13, for the Eastern team's only loss of the season, while the *New York Times* marveled at "the most sensational football ever seen in the East."

In his autobiography, Rockne claimed that this victory over Army was the reason for "the development of Notre Dame spirit." The entire faculty and student body met the team in what was the first of hundreds of wild greetings to come. Said Rockne, "It brought out more boys for varsity football—and began attracting high school players who might have gone elsewhere."

Following graduation, thanks to Coach Harper and Father Nieuwland, Rockne accepted a $2,400 offer to work at Notre Dame as a combination chemistry teacher and assistant football coach. Almost from the start of practice, noted the coach's biographer Jerry Brondfield, Rockne demonstrated skill as a strategist. He emphasized the importance of breaking away on the snap to the Irish ends and invented what came to be known as the Notre Dame shift. The secret to the shift was pinpoint timing; the ball needed to be snapped before the defense could react. Rockne said the shift offense created a "new and artistic game," and he compared the strategy to the "flank movement in warfare."

"Let's flex the ends along with the backs," said Rockne. "Put one or both of them out 2, 3, or 4 yards as needed. It will mask our real point of attack, give us more momentum, and get as many men as possible to that point on every play."[2]

Rockne became Harper's righthand man. In 1918, when the head coach departed Notre Dame to take over a relative's ranch in Kansas, he persuaded Notre Dame's president, Father John Cavanaugh, to offer the thirty-year-old Rockne the job. The salary of $5,000 per year seemed perfect to the new coach, who had married Bonnie Skiles of Sandusky, Ohio, in July 1914. From day one on the job, Rockne made it his mission to establish Notre Dame as a national sports power, and he succeeded by developing winning teams and by charming all with his salesmanship. Never before or since has a nation so identified one coach with one college, as Rockne and Notre Dame were linked.

Rockne, a professor as well as a coach, quickly proved to be an intelligent tactician. "Handling your personnel is the most important phase of coaching," he told one sportswriter. "The secret of coaching success can be reduced to a simple formula: strict discipline in your training program and on the field, combined with a high and continuing interest in all your other relationships with your kids."

Concluded Rockne, "We can all be geniuses because one definition of genius is the infinite capacity for taking pains. Perfection in petty detail is most essential."[3]

Rockne proved to be the most successful coach ever to use emotion as a tool for winning. Relying on his brassy voice, which could become intense enough to sweep cobwebs from the ceiling in an instant, the coach routinely exhorted his team to come from behind at halftime. His most famous halftime oration was his "Win one for the Gipper" speech.

George Gipp was a Notre Dame freshman who was

thinking about dropping out of school when Knute Rockne discovered the young man dropkicking 50-yard field goals on a university lawn. Rockne invited the solemn-looking youth to a freshman practice, and the recruit responded by running for a touchdown in his first play. In his first season, Gipp kicked a 62-yard field goal against Western State Normal, defeated Indiana with a slashing touchdown run, and produced 480 total yards against Army.

But as Gipp's biographer, Patrick Chelland, pointed out, the player was an off-the-field maverick, notorious for gambling on Notre Dame games and cutting classes. Still, there was something about Gipp that Rockne and his teammates loved. For one thing, he was a winner.

Gipp died of complications due to pneumonia during the 1920 season. Although seriously ill, he threw two passes for long touchdowns against Northwestern in his final game for Notre Dame.

Eight years later, as the Irish battled a seemingly invincible Army team, Rockne shook his team with a quiet locker room speech that was immortalized by sportswriter Grantland Rice. "I've got to go, Rock," said Rockne, imitating the dying man's gestures. "It's all right. I'm not afraid. Sometime, Rock, when things are wrong and the breaks are beating the boys, tell them to go in there with all they've got and win one just for the Gipper. I don't know where I'll be then, Rock, but I'll know about it. And I'll be happy."

The Irish ran out of the room and played hardnosed football. The final score was 12–6 in Notre Dame's favor, and the New York *Daily News* ran perhaps its most famous headline: *Gipp's Ghost Beat Army*.

Rockne never used the same speech twice on his lads. He had a showman's instinct for when he should demonstrate anger, when he should exhort, when he should stick in the needle, when he should hold his silence, and even when he should stretch the truth. There is the famous story about the time his team won a big game for his son who was sick in the hospital, only to learn later the boy was as healthy as a horse. One time he simply stuck his round head into the locker room after a dreadful first half. "I beg your pardon," he said icily. "I thought this was a Notre Dame team." Another time, he abandoned his stalled team to sit up in the stands until his provoked charges took their anger out on the opposition.

But Rockne relied on more than mere gimmickry to succeed. He was a pioneer in scientific analysis, and he believed in giving his teams every technological advantage. If not the first, then he was one of the first to film his players during practice, to look for tendencies and flaws in technique. He scouted the enemy before all games, considering such preparation to be the coach's equivalent of academic research. He attended theatrical rehearsals, reported sportswriter Edwin Pope, "to find out how tempo and interest were maintained in the choruses," then "went back to practice and mapped out frequent breaks and faster drills."[4] Occasionally, he started his second-string players—called the Shock Troop—using them to slow down the opposition and give the enemy false confidence, before sending in the fresh first team.

While George Gipp was Rockne's most famous player, without doubt his most famous team was the one with a backfield composed of Jim Crowley, Don Miller, Elmer Layden, and Harry Stuhldreher. Grantland Rice immortalized these players with a biblical reference to them in his column for the New York *Herald Tribune*. That column, written to celebrate an Irish 13–7 win, contained this famous line: "Outlined against a blue-gray October sky, the Four Horsemen rode again."

Quick to use the media to his advantage, Rockne ordered his four star players to climb aboard a local farmer's nags and thus produced the most famous public relations photograph in the history of college sports. The 1924 team went undefeated in the regular season and smashed Stanford in the Rose Bowl, 27–10. All of the

Horsemen, save Miller, were named consensus All-Americans. During his career, the coach developed fifteen All-American players, truly an impressive total.

At the end of that glorious season, Knute Rockne took religious instruction and converted to the Catholic Church. This move alone made him so popular at Notre Dame that, if he weren't married, Irish fans might have campaigned for him to become the next pope.

The 1924 season catapulted Rockne to the same degree of fame that sports heroes Jack Dempsey and Babe Ruth enjoyed. The *Cleveland Press* called him the Buffalo Bill of his generation. He and his attractive wife Bonnie enjoyed a happy marriage marred only by his frequent absences, and the couple reared four children. The only serious illness the coach had to endure was an attack of phlebitis in 1929, which forced him to attend games in a wheelchair. Perhaps the most touching moment in sports history occurred in 1929, when Rockne defied his doctor's orders and the potentially fatal blood clot in his body to deliver a stirring oration before the Carnegie Tech game— a game the Irish had lost 27–7 the previous season. "Why do you think I'm taking a chance like this?" he yelled. "To see you lose?" The players looked with horror at a man they feared would die in front of them. "Fight to live," he shouted. "Fight to win. Fight to live. Fight to win, win, *win!*"

Notre Dame defeated Carnegie Tech 7–0 in one of Rockne's most treasured victories.

Nothing slowed him down. He traveled the country, delivering speeches and making celebrity guest appearances to augment his Notre Dame salary. While on the road lecturing or recruiting athletes, he frequently stopped at high schools where former players coached. Within minutes his coat was off as he chalked X's and O's on a blackboard. Rockne was always willing to discuss strategy.

If any man was on top of the world, it was Knute Rockne. Notre Dame had built him a magnificent stadium the previous year, and both his 1929 (9–0–0) and 1930 (10–0–0) teams experienced undefeated seasons. But on March 31, 1931, flying from Kansas City to Los Angeles aboard Transcontinental Western's Flight 599 to participate in the grand opening of a sporting goods chain and make a football demonstration movie, Rockne watched ice form on the wings of the small plane in which he was flying. Unlike the episode as a boy when he was rescued off the ice, no one could save Rockne this time. The plane crashed in a wheat field near Bazaar, Kansas. Eight passengers, including Rockne, perished. Ironically, the accident occurred only a few miles from Jesse Harper's ranch. The man who gave Knute Rockne the only big break he ever needed was called in to positively identify the shattered remains.

As a measure of his fame, the Studebaker motor company named an automobile after him, the Rockne Six. The U.S. government named a Liberty ship, the *S.S. Knute Rockne,* after him, too. But no one could do what every teary-eyed American wanted to do when they heard the news of the great man's death. No one could bring him back.

5

BUD WILKINSON: *SEMPER PARATIS*

Charles Burnham "Bud" Wilkinson began his head coaching duties at the University of Oklahoma when he was only thirty-one, but not even his fiercest critic ever could accuse him of immaturity. He ran his squads with an iron hand but was usually even-tempered and unemotional in times of both victory and defeat. "You can motivate players better with kind words than you can with a whip," he used to preach. "Football success is desire and speed and intelligence—and desire is 85 percent of it."

During his seventeen-year tenure with the Sooners, Wilkinson's teams boasted a collegiate record of 145 wins, 29 losses, and 4 ties, a phenomenal winning percentage of .833. Wilkinson led Oklahoma to three national championships, fourteen conference titles, and the longest winning streak (forty-seven consecutive games) in college football history. If he hadn't turned his back upon college football for an unsuccessful bid at a political career, Wilkinson, in all likelihood, would have won more cumulative victories than any other college head coach.

Born on April 23, 1916, in the city of Minneapolis, Wilkinson grew up in a well-to-do environment. Charles P. Wilkinson, his father, was a banker and successful entrepreneur.

Young Bud attended the Shattuck School—a prep

school for the wealthy—in Faribault, Minnesota, participating in a drama group and five varsity sports. Although he reached nearly his final height and weight of 6 feet-1 inch, 190 pounds, while still in prep school, Wilkinson did not bloom fully as an athlete until he made the University of Minnesota Gophers' hockey, golf, and football teams as a lowly walk-on.

At Minnesota, Wilkinson became the big man on campus, both for his athletic talent and for his clean-cut good looks that caused sportswriters to label him "the golden man of the gridiron." He played goalie on the Gophers' Big Ten Conference championship hockey teams in 1934 and 1935, making team captain in his junior year. He also lettered in golf and scored in the low eighties.

The future coach was no slouch in the classroom either. An English major, he received the Big Ten Conference Medal in 1937 for the best combined record in athletics and scholarship. Later in life, Wilkinson told the *New York Times* that he believed football should always play second fiddle to a player's studies. "There is no great intellectual gain in football," said Wilkinson. "The aim of football is or should be the aim of the university—to develop talent to the highest degree."

But it was in football, not in academia, where Wilkinson gained lasting fame. He was fortunate to attend college when the Gophers dominated the Big Ten (then known as the Western Conference) from 1934 to 1936. He starred under highly regarded head coach Bernard "Bernie" Bierman, a man with looks as hard as a Minnesota winter, who influenced Wilkinson as both a person and strategist. "Bernie's the greatest football coach I've ever known—a molder of character and a great man," Wilkinson told writer Francis Wallace.

In the snowy-haired Bierman's career at Minnesota from 1932 to 1941 and 1945 to 1950, his Gophers won five national championships and six Big Ten titles. It was said of Bierman, with only slight hyperbole, that he "never lost his temper, never raised his voice, never shed a tear, never appealed to sentiment, [and] never played sentimental tricks on his team."[1]

Bud Wilkinson learned both composure under pressure and the value of physical conditioning from his mentor. Years later, Wilkinson taught his lessons by draping a long arm over a player's shoulder, not by angry outbursts, except while exhorting someone to get into shape. "Run, run, run!" he'd yell both before and after his practice scrimmages, putting emphasis upon performing 10-yard sprints in those days before aerobic exercises became popular.

In 1935, Coach Bierman converted Wilkinson from guard to quarterback, certainly one of the few such successful metamorphoses in the history of college ball. The new quarterback took Minnesota to an 8–0–0 season with one of the greatest teams of all time, featuring swift Andy Uram at halfback, Frank Larson at end, and All-American Bill Bevan at guard. Wilkinson also played on the 1936 team, which had the misfortune to lose to the Northwestern Wildcats, 6–0, ending the Gophers' twenty-eight game unbeaten streak going back to 1933. Nonetheless, thanks to the determined play of Wilkinson as quarterback and All-American tackle Ed Widseth, the Gophers were named national champions in 1936, by both the Associated Press (AP) and United Press International (UPI).

Following graduation, in 1937, Wilkinson worked one summer under his father, but the gridiron soon beckoned him again. He accepted a position at Syracuse as an assistant coach, earning an M.A. in English and education in four years. He married his University of Minnesota girlfriend, Mary Shifflett, in August 1938, a union that lasted thirty-seven years and produced two sons. During World War II, he served in the U.S. Navy.

Ironically, Wilkinson made his most important coaching contact while in military service. Stationed for a time at the Iowa Preflight School, he worked as an assistant coach under former University of Missouri coach Don Faurot.

Faurot, in short order, convinced his new pupil to appreciate the intricacies of the split-T formation, an offensive attack that Faurot had invented but that Wilkinson was destined to popularize. Years later, in an interview with famed New York sports columnist Arthur Daley, Wilkinson admitted that Faurot "taught me everything I know about football."

Essentially, players in the split-T formation lined up as shown in the illustration below.

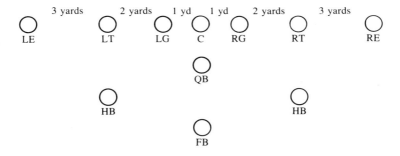

Instead of playing shoulder-to-shoulder, as was customary, the offensive line left intentional gaps between players. The ends lined up 3 yards away from the tackles. The tackles lined up 2 yards away from the guards. The guards lined up 1 yard away from the center. The center, quarterback, and fullback lined up behind one another, while the two halfbacks lined up directly behind the tackles. The success of the split-T depended upon having a quarterback who could run and throw, because the wide gaps in the line forced the quarterback to select only play-action calls.

Still, for years enemy defenses found it difficult to adjust to the revolutionary wide splits in this offense. Only after defensive linemen and linebackers began shooting the gap through these splits did the split-T meet its match, but even so, Wilkinson overcame such innovations in defense by changing his offense from a ball-control game to an aerial attack, as well as by alternating the direction of blocks.

One of Wilkinson's favorite plays off the split-T was a fullback counter. The halfbacks and quarterback faked two steps left. The quarterback then pivoted and handed off to the fullback. After the quarterback handed off, he faced the offense and faked a forward pass. The fullback stepped to the right of the quarterback and squeezed between the center and right guard. Important blocking assignments were given the right guard, who took on the guard opposite him; the center and left guard, who double-teamed the offensive guard; and the right tackle, who cross-blocked the linebacker.[2]

Wilkinson's tutelage under Faurot lasted only one season, but the knowledge he gained lasted his whole career. The young officer soon shipped out aboard the carrier *Enterprise* to find action at Iwo Jima, Tokyo, and Okinawa. His military obligation ended in 1945.

After the service, Wilkinson accepted his father's invitation to join him at his Minneapolis bank. But when University of Oklahoma coach Jim Tatum offered him a position as an assistant, Wilkinson said he "stopped kidding" himself about a business career and moved to the tiny Oklahoma town of Norman. "There's nothing like football except going to war—and people get killed going to war," he often said, explaining the game's attraction for him.

After enjoying an 8–3 season and winning the Gator Bowl against North Carolina State University in 1946, Tatum found himself in trouble with Oklahoma president George Cross. Cross charged that Tatum had spent $6,000 on cash gifts for team members, a decision clearly in violation of NCAA rules.[3] Before any action could be taken, however, Tatum became head coach and athletic director at the University of Maryland, a move that resulted in Wilkinson's big coaching break much sooner than he ever imagined.

Wilkinson's 1947 season—which the team entered with a sixteenth place ranking in the AP poll—was nearly his last. The Sooners went 2–2–1 in the first five games, and the howls of alumni calling for his scalp forced him to take drastic action. He benched his starters, mostly returning servicemen with priorities other than football to consider, and won his last five games of the season with youngsters such as Darrell Royal, destined to become a top coach himself at the University of Texas.

Despite this successful first year, alumni grumblings sounded again at season's end until Navy offered its vacant head coaching job to Wilkinson. Convinced of Wilkinson's worth because someone else wanted him, Oklahoma offered him an attractive new contract that made him both coach and athletic director. With perks such as a weekly television show, royalties from two books on football, lectures, and coaching clinics to augment his $20,000 salary, it was estimated in 1954 that his income was $102,000—a whopping figure in those years.

After surviving his shaky first year, Wilkinson became an Oklahoma legend, winning three national championships and six bowl games in seventeen seasons as head coach. The Sooners were the pride of the Big Seven, finishing first every season from 1948 through 1959 and losing just one of seventy games over that span. Because of such domination, when Oklahoma State was added to the conference in 1960, the league earned the dubious title of "Oklahoma and the Seven Dwarfs."

Wilkinson always insisted that he loved what he did for a living. "I never got up in the morning when I felt I was going to work," he told *Collier's* magazine, "and that's a grand way to feel about making a living."

The coach was one of the first in his profession to insist that athletes could be scholars. With the Sooners, he graduated 92 percent of his players. Because the cream of America's youth played at Oklahoma, Sooners' president Dr. George Cross voiced his now-famous quip: "We want a freshman class here that our football team can be proud of." Wilkinson also stressed clean living, insisting that drinking is a chink in a player's moral armor. He himself unwound by listening to classical music and playing bridge.

The secrets to Wilkinson's success were his insistence upon organization, well-run practices, and a positive mental attitude. He favored maintaining first and second units for both offense and defense, and he substituted units instead of individuals. By recruiting well-conditioned athletes and keeping them at their physical peak throughout a season, Oklahoma simply overpowered the opposition. The Sooners' time-of-possession frequently amounted to three-fourths of a game.

Wilkinson preached that his chain of players was no stronger than the weakest link. "We try to create the atmosphere that the last boy on our squad is as important as the number-one boy," he once said. "That's why we spend so much time with the boys who play on the lower units."

One reason that Wilkinson could spend so much time with his players was that his thin-as-rawhide frame required little sleep. On a typical summer's workday, he rose between 4 and 5 A.M., driving himself nonstop for up to seventeen hours. To combat the Oklahoma heat, he sandwiched his day between two-hour workouts that began at 6:30 A.M. and 4:30 P.M. In between he discussed strategy with his staff, reviewed films, and held meetings with his players. "He organizes his schedule like a bank robber," one friend told writer William Barry Furlong.

Bud Wilkinson

Wilkinson estimated that six to twelve hours of coaching preparation went into one hour of practice. If his sessions had a fault, it was that players occasionally found them monotonous. Nonetheless, Oklahoma men seldom lost games due to poor blocking or tackling, because he perpetually stressed fundamentals. He often tried players out at up to five different positions, seeking to find the best position for each man.

A master at drawing up an unexpected game plan for big games, he deviated from his usual crunching offense against conference archrival Nebraska in 1962. The coach launched an air attack behind quarterback Monte Deere to score three touchdowns by passing en route to a 34–6 win. "We were concerned with their running game," groaned Nebraska coach Bob Devaney. "We should have shot the air out of the football."

Wilkinson was in the midst of a prosperous career at Oklahoma. But the pressures of trying to field a national champion year after year, combined with having to take over the family business due to the recent deaths of his father and brother, suddenly made something snap inside him. In January 1964, he resigned from Oklahoma, altered his political allegiance from Democrat to Republican, and announced his candidacy for a seat in the U.S. Senate. But, as it turned out, Wilkinson had overestimated the value of an outstanding coaching career in the public's mind. He lost to Fred R. Harris in a close race, and with that loss returned to running the family business.

Leaving Oklahoma in the midst of a flourishing career was not the biggest mistake Wilkinson made as a football coach. His worst decision was to return to the game in 1978 when, at the request of St. Louis owner Bill Bidwell, he assumed control of the hapless Cardinals of the National Football League. Observers believed Wilkinson's decision was motivated by financial reversals, most notably a hefty divorce settlement awarded Mary.

Ralph Neely of the Dallas Cowboys, a former Wilkinson star at Oklahoma, said publicly after the signing that his old coach could not possibly succeed because "the game has changed so much in the last fifteen years." But Wilkinson pooh-poohed such criticism, pointing out that the 1978 Cards relied on the popular 3–4 defense. "Shucks, all the 3–4 is is a variation on the Oklahoma Defense that I invented thirty years ago."[4]

However, it turned out that time and the game *had* passed Wilkinson by. Sadly, at age sixty-three, he was dismissed in the second year of his contract, after the Cardinals had lost their first eight games, ending up 9–20 under him. The coach refused to criticize his owner, but he did blame his poor record on the team's failure to sign quality players. "If you're going to make chicken salad, then you better begin with chicken," he told the press.

Thus ended the coaching career of the man so often called a football legend. But Wilkinson remained in the game for years to come, using his lifetime of knowledge in a new career as a sports broadcaster.

6

VINCE LOMBARDI: MAKING A DYNASTY OUT OF FORMER LOSERS

Vince Lombardi was the Leo Durocher of professional football, insisting that nice guys finish last. He was a boss who drove his charges like mules, and he was a master at squeezing the last bit of talent from rookies and veterans alike.

Bob Oates, a staff writer for the *Los Angeles Times*, rated Lombardi the greatest coach ever to stalk the gridiron. Certainly, many of the coach's players and opponents would agree. Other coaches may have won more games in their careers, but Lombardi dominated the sport like no man before or since has ever done. During his nine seasons at Green Bay, he took a bunch of perennial losers and shaped them ruthlessly into a world-famous powerhouse. "He treated us all the same," claimed rugged Henry Jordan, Lombardi's longtime defensive tackle, "like dogs."

But Lombardi's tactics always paid off in victories. His teams won 75 percent of their games and five National Football League championships. His Packers won two Super Bowl rings and never experienced a losing season. His twenty-year career with Green Bay and the Washington Redskins produced an enviable .738 winning percentage. "Winning isn't everything—it's the only thing" is the credo he lived by, even though, contrary to published reports, he didn't originate that famous saying.

There was no great secret to Lombardi's successes. He used his mind, not his heart, to make what some observers considered cold-blooded decisions about his personnel. There was no room for sentiment in his assessment of his players. Even giant linemen feared him. He insisted on obedience and discipline. Any Packer who played the role of prodigal son found him an unforgiving father figure.

Nor did Lombardi take his players' skills for granted. He preached basics and forced his charges to practice fundamentals until they dropped. His philosophy was that the harder you work, the harder it is to surrender. As a result, not only did his teams rarely kick away games on turnovers, but they knew how to force less disciplined opponents into coughing up the football. They blocked better, tackled harder, and played better than their big-name opponents did.

"Teams do not go physically stale," Lombardi preached. "They go mentally stale."[1]

Of all the great coaches featured in this book, Lombardi was the latest to bloom. Born in Brooklyn, New York, on June 11, 1913, he was the epitome of the tough street kid. Matilda and Harry, his mother and father, were Italian immigrants of the Catholic faith. Harry Lombardi was a butcher with a loyal following in the neighborhood. He believed that his young son needed to learn work habits early. Therefore, he insisted that Vince work after school, keeping the shop spic and span.

The Lombardi family wasn't dirt poor, but money was tight enough for Harry to dress his son in mended knickerbockers and turned-around shirt collars. The elder Lombardi merely tolerated Vince's love for this brutal American game called football. Once, when his son tried to beg off work because of a leg injured in a game, his father showed a temper that his legendary son learned to emulate. Harry said something to Vince at that time that made a lasting impression. "Hurt is in your mind," said the elder Lombardi. (Later in life, Lombardi told sportswriter Gene Schoor, "You've got to make yourself tough and you've got to play when it hurts. That's when you play best, when it hurts.")[2]

After that incident with his father, Vince Lombardi played with pain. Later, with the Packers, the volatile coach demanded his players do the same. "All hurt is in the mind," he'd tell them.

Curiously, Lombardi's first choice of profession was the priesthood. For three years he attended a junior seminary before deciding that he did not have a religious calling. When St. Francis Preparatory School, a Brooklyn football power, offered the boy a full scholarship in the midst of the Great Depression, he accepted.

The coach at St. Francis was Harry Kane, a short and rotund man whose appearance belied his talent as a knowledgeable sportsman. When Kane coached at Commerce High School before coming to St. Francis, he had helped develop Lou Gehrig's talents as a football and baseball player.

Lombardi proved an eager pupil. From Kane he learned the importance of teamwork. Kane stressed the execution of blocking and tackling fundamentals, as well as the importance of knowing where one's teammates were on every play. Lombardi—only 5 feet-8 inches tall and 160 pounds—was as aggressive as a young stallion, happiest when "trading" forearms with an opponent. In his first year as a player, Lombardi was named All-City Catholic High School Fullback, leading St. Francis to the City Catholic High School Championship.

Lombardi was a straight-A student who impressed Dan Kern, his Greek teacher, in the classroom as well as on the gridiron. Kern, a Fordham University alumnus, convinced his alma mater to give the kid from Brooklyn a football scholarship. In his letter of recommendation, Kern called his honor student "the broadest, toughest, most aggressive ballplayer I've ever seen."

Lombardi played at Fordham from 1934 to 1938. His

teammates nicknamed him "Butch," but he was better known as one of the famed "Seven Blocks of Granite," as sportswriter Tim Cohane of *Look* magazine named the school's 1935–36 offensive line. Fordham's coach, Jim Crowley, had played in Knute Rockne's backfield at Notre Dame, winning everlasting fame as a member of the "Four Horsemen" backfield. Crowley, naturally enough, stressed the importance of perfecting one's assignments. He believed that a team with impeccable timing and precision defense would stop more powerful opponents every time.

Lombardi was shifted to the guard position and impressed Crowley with his indomitable spirit. In one victory against mighty Pittsburgh, Lombardi played an entire game despite the loss of several teeth and a cut cheek that took thirty stitches to repair. "I remember sitting in that Polo Grounds dressing room during halftime," Lombardi later recalled, "and it felt like every tooth in my head was loose."

After graduation, Lombardi attended law school until Andy Palau, a teammate of his with the Fordham Rams, offered him a combination teaching and assistant coaching position at St. Cecilia High School in Englewood, New Jersey. Palau and his assistant taught their students the Notre Dame system that Crowley had passed onto them. In his first year as an assistant, with the line as his main responsibility, Lombardi earned his first taste of future glory. St. Cecilia won not only the Englewood city championship but also the New Jersey private school championship.

When Palau left St. Cecilia in 1942 to become an assistant at Fordham, Lombardi made the most of his opportunity. He scrapped Palau's Notre Dame system in favor of the newfangled T-formation popularized by the Chicago Bears. After losing the first game due to inexperience, Lombardi's team in the next three years won thirty games, tied two, and lost none. One of the proudest members of the 1944 team was the coach's younger brother, Joseph, who was one of seven St. Cecilia players named to the All-County Eleven.

Even at the high school level Lombardi was an innovator. It was at St. Cecilia that he originated what came to be known as his "run to daylight" offense. Other coaches wanted players to block a particular defensive player while the running back plowed through a specific hole. But with Lombardi's way—his technique perfected years later at Green Bay—the linemen blocked an area; the backs waited until a hole opened either to the inside or outside, and then they split the gap.

Vince Lombardi's success earned him a bid to join then-coach Ed Danowski at Fordham in 1947. Unfortunately, the two men clashed, and Lombardi jumped at an opportunity to join the staff of Colonel Earl "Red" Blaik at West Point. From Blaik, Lombardi learned many axioms that helped during his glory years. "There is no substitute for work," said Blaik, who expected his coaches to put in seventeen-hour days. "It is the price of success."[3]

Lombardi was as happy in his five years at West Point as he was miserable at Fordham. "The most important thing that ever happened to me in football was the opportunity to coach under Coach Blaik," he once wrote. "Whatever success I have had must be attributed to 'the old man.' He molded my methods and my whole approach to the game."

In 1954, Lombardi left Blaik to become an assistant coach with the New York Giants. Five years later, the hapless Green Bay Packers offered him a job as head coach. Thus, at the age of forty-one, Vince Lombardi began a career that would ultimately make the man into a legend.

At Green Bay, Lombardi was like a Western hero walking into a town that needed help fast. "I hold it more important to have the players' confidence than their affection," he declared. The Packers of 1958 were a mixture of the inept, the lazy, and the careless. His first move was to clean out the malingerers hanging around the trainer's room for rubdowns and whirlpool baths.

His father's voice must have spoken between his ears as he ordered them to ignore their minor hurts. "He'd say, 'You can't hurt a charley horse,' " fullback Jim Taylor later reminisced in Jerry Kramer's book *Lombardi*. "And even if it hurt, even if you were suffering some pain, he instilled in you the feeling that you couldn't get reinjured."

The next day, when Lombardi visited the trainer's room, only two severely injured players were present. Later, during training camp, he ranted insanely at two veterans who tried to party their way to opening day, and rumors said he had tattooed a wall with one offender's head.

"I've got all the emotions in excess, and a hair trigger controls them," he later would confess. Needless to say, the Packers learned to respect him or left to join a new team.

Lombardi's strategies were more complicated than many sportswriters believed them to be. He revolved his offense around a former All-American and Heisman Trophy winner from Notre Dame, Paul Hornung, whose nickname of the Golden Boy reflected his uninhibited off-the-field lifestyle. The coach's first brilliant move was to convert Hornung from a so-so quarterback into a half-back, a decision that eventually would put the Golden Boy into the Hall of Fame. Having a former quarterback in Hornung gave the Packers an important pass option. In one game against Baltimore in 1965, Hornung scored a record five touchdowns. Lombardi used to boast that inside the 20-yard line, his halfback could actually smell the goal line.

The coach—who also had absolute control as the team's general manager—seemed to have an equally good nose for sniffing talent. He gave a first-string assignment to Fred "Fuzzy" Thurston, who had failed in tryouts in Chicago, Philadelphia, and Baltimore, but who blossomed into an

All-Pro starting guard under Lombardi. He took seriously a letter from a skinny nobody named Willie Wood from the University of Southern California, who begged for a shot at pro ball. Wood, of course, was to become one of the best punt return men in the history of the game, as well as a glue-handed demon of a free safety.

On his door Lombardi hung a sign that read *Mr. Lombardi* instead of *Coach*. He demanded respect and received it in a hurry. He also proved to be a clever horse trader, obtaining tackle Henry Jordan, halfback Lew Carpenter, end Willie Davis, and defensive end Bill Quinlan from the talent-rich Browns in exchange for no players of consequence.

Lombardi made a household name out of Bart Starr who, until that time, had toiled as a Packer backup quarterback. Football, according to Lombardi, was a running game. The pass was intended to keep the defense guessing, he said, and ball control was the key to victory. But Lombardi also promised Starr the protection a quarterback needed to stay alive behind the line of scrimmage, let alone be effective. The coach and his assistants worked on plays that kept Starr safely in the pocket.

Lombardi ran a modified T-formation that depended upon two-man blocking to open a hole that gained runners 3 yards and a cloud of dust. He also made stars out of pulling guards such as Thurston and Jerry Kramer, who, on the coach's famed 49-sweep around end, opened those holes for Hornung and Jim Taylor to plow through.

The beauty of the sweep was that Lombardi kept it flexible. Hornung, for example, had the option to throw if he found the hole plugged. And both Hornung and Taylor were free to skirt through an inside hole if one materialized. Lombardi was years ahead of his time in

Vince Lombardi

anticipating the tendencies of the defense, assigning his assistant Phil Bengston to figure out how individual opponents might try to halt the power sweep.

Another play that Lombardi's Packers executed well was the kickoff. In his book, *Run to Daylight* (1963), the coach revealed his philosophy on this particular play, noting that size is as important as speed on the kickoff team. "You need that size, particularly in the middle to meet their wedge, and you put your two real speed burners as the third men in from either sideline," wrote Lombardi. "They are the ones who have to force the action, who must make the other [side] show their play, and your two outside men have to be strong enough and active enough to keep that play to the inside. Those outside men have got to stay upright and protect those sidelines, but they can't be so sideline-conscious that they just stand around out there like a couple of program venders."

Lombardi's strategies brought immediate success to Green Bay, which had finished the season under Ray "Scooter" McLean in 1958 with a dismal 1–10–1 record, the worst season since the team began in 1919. Before the new coach's arrival, one witty sportswriter had dubbed the Packers the Conga team, because, he said, all their offense amounted to was 1–2–3 kick, 1–2–3 kick.

In his first season at Green Bay, Lombardi's Packers shocked the sports world, which had come to look upon the team as the league's doormat. The Packers opened the season by defeating the Chicago Bears, their fellow rival from the north, 9–6, and won the next two games to boot. After a midseason slump that had Lombardi frothing at the mouth, the Packers came back to finish with a 7–5 record, and the freshman headmaster earned Coach of the Year honors.

This was the start of the famed Packer dynasty that saw Lombardi's men win NFL titles in 1961, 1962, 1965, 1966, and 1967. In addition, the Packers won Super Bowl I and Super Bowl II played in 1967 and 1968, respectively.

The first win against the upstart American Football

League (AFL) was especially satisfying. Kansas City head coach Hank Stram had brought his Chiefs the AFL title partly on the strength of his baffling playbook. Unlike the grind-it-out tactics of Lombardi, Stram preferred such daring formations as triple stack defenses, shifts, tight-end I's, and various man-in-motion plays.

It took Lombardi until halftime to figure out his enemy. The coach stormed into the dressing room with the Packers nursing a scant 14–10 lead over the underdog Chiefs. A fired-up Packers team emerged to start the third quarter. Linebacker Dave Robinson stormed Kansas City quarterback Len Dawson on a blitz, resulting in an errant pass that Willie Wood ran back 40 yards to the Chiefs' 5-yard line. Elijah Pitts carried the ball into the end zone on the next play for a 21–10 Green Bay lead.

From that point on, the Packers excelled. Bart Starr used his ground game as Lombardi had mandated, but he also drilled flanker Max McGee with a flurry of short passes after realizing Kansas City cornerback Willie Mitchell was playing too far back off the line. Late in the third quarter, McGee outwitted Mitchell in the end zone to catch a 13-yard toss for a 28–10 lead. The Packers added a fourth touchdown in the final quarter for a 35–10 lead, and at that point Lombardi relied on his ground attack to run down the clock.

The next year a similar slaughter of the AFL was anticipated as Green Bay met the Oakland Raiders. But at halftime the score was close, 16–7, and after Lombardi had finished stripping the paint off the clubhouse wall with another spirited tirade, Jerry Kramer took the floor. "Let's play the last thirty minutes for the old man," he shouted, pointing to Lombardi. "All of us love him. Let's not let him down."

A rejuvenated bunch of Packer old-timers retook the field and ended Oakland's hopes at 33–14. Kramer and Forrest Gregg lifted Lombardi onto their shoulders for what proved to be the last time.

The head coach moved to Washington for the 1969

season and ended his career the way he had begun it, with a 7–5–2 season. But the old man finally met an enemy he couldn't lick—intestinal cancer. On July 26, 1970, Vince Lombardi left his hospital bed to watch his Redskin rookies play the Baltimore Colts' rookies. He marched into the dressing room and announced, "It's great to be here with my team."

But he would never coach again. On September 3, 1970, time ran out on him. He died at Georgetown University Hospital.

7

PAUL BROWN: THE BRAINTRUST

During his forty-five year career as a coach with teams on the high school, college, military, and professional level, Paul Brown consistently demonstrated his winning ways. Brown's professional career began in 1946 in the All-American Football Conference with the Cleveland Browns, where his teams won four consecutive league championships. In 1950, the Browns moved to the National Football League, and the coach once again led them to a league championship. In thirteen NFL seasons, he won seven divisional titles and three league championships.

Paul Brown, Ohio's favorite son, was born in 1908 in Norwalk, a small town an hour's drive from Cleveland, and his family moved when he was nine to Massillon. Brown typified the Midwest values of his native state. His father, Lester, was a railroad dispatcher, and his mother, Ida, was a housewife who loved to play cards with her son when he came home from school.

In his autobiography, *PB: The Paul Brown Story* (1979), the coach admitted that his fondness for precision plays reflected his father's influence. As a railroad dispatcher, Lester Brown made decisions that affected the well-being of passengers. He needed to be meticulous and demanding to perform his job—two character traits that Paul inherited in abundance. Lester prepared his son for the college education he never had by giving him pennies and nickels for performing odd jobs, all of which went into the boy's toy lion bank. His father bought Paul his first football at age six. When the bladder burst from overuse, the boy filled it with leaves and kept using it.

Brown was not the only Massillon boy bitten by the football bug. The city had sponsored football games that were amateur in name only since the 1890s. Because local businesses offered attractive purses to its team, even true professional players sometimes joined the Massillon Tigers to play rivals in Akron and Canton. As a boy, Brown used to sneak into as many games as he could. Significantly, Brown was one of five boys from his old neighborhood to end up as a football coach, although none of the others approached his own successes. His gang gathered as early as 7 A.M. to scrounge up a game.

Outside of his father, Brown's major influence while growing up was his coach at Massillon High, Dave Stewart, a wiry man just out of college himself. At first, Stewart thought this skinny, 120-pound stick of a boy had no talent for football and listed him as a fifth-string quarterback. But the coach underestimated young Brown's determination. In his first game as a substitute, the sophomore youngster threw a touchdown on his first career pass. A year later, he started at quarterback and also starred in basketball, track, and baseball. Stewart taught Brown that coaching was nothing more than an extension of classroom teaching, and the future coach of the Cleveland Browns believed in this philosophy his whole life. "For me, teaching became an obsession as it related to my coaching," he once admitted. On the personal side, he fell in love with an attractive brown-haired woman named Katy Kester, who was destined to become his bride. The two shared a love for milkshakes and boat outings.

Brown started college at Ohio State University, but the size of the school overwhelmed the homesick boy, and he transferred to Miami University in the tiny southwestern Ohio town of Oxford. Weeb Ewbank, who would become an assistant coach at Cleveland for Brown following the end of World War II, was the Miami quarterback whom he replaced. He also punted and returned punts.

Brown quickly showed that he had the heart of a gambler by throwing bombs on first down and fake-punting before running the ball. Much later, as a pro coach, he drove teams mad by calling unexpected plays. Also, although it was against school rules, he secretly married Katy on June 10, 1929, a full year before his graduation.

Brown's career began rather ordinarily. He taught and coached at Severn Prep, a small Annapolis, Maryland, school for two years, compiling a 16-1 record. His reward was a $1,600 head coaching position at Massillon High School, where he remained for nine years and won 80 games, including his final 33 in a row. Part of Brown's strategy was that he believed that you won games only if you had athletes. He cut inferior players immediately, demanding that his players possess what he called the four absolutes: speed, intelligence, agility, and the ability to assimilate football plays. As a result, on the high school and later the college level, Brown's squads possessed fewer players than did those of other coaches.

"There is no point in scrimmaging a boy you know is not going to make your team," Brown told Jack Clary, author of *The Gamemakers* (1976), a book on contemporary coaches. "There is no need to bruise him and no need for you to waste your time on him. I would rather concentrate my time on the players who will be with me during the season."

Brown, in particular, tried to develop relationships with his quarterbacks. A boy couldn't play the position for him unless he could both think and throw. A player with a powerful arm who lacked the ability to call plays was a liability on the field. One of the coach's rituals was to walk up and down an empty football field with his quarterback, asking him what play he would call in this situation or that. He demanded that his signal caller visualize ahead of time what his team might come up against.

Even at the high school level, the young coach quickly became known as an innovator. At Massillon, he was the only high school coach to use playbooks, requiring players to write down in a three-ring binder plays and formations. Later in his career, he introduced the practice on the college level at Ohio State and on the professional level at Cleveland. At first his opponents made fun of the practice, saying that it "sissified" the sport. But when Brown's well-schooled teams continued to annihilate all competition, rival coaches began to adopt playbooks as a matter of course.

Brown was one of the first great coaches to emphasize fundamentals for both experienced and rookie players. Players used blocking sleds three times a week and were required to execute fifty hits each time. "Great emphasis was placed on the offensive and defensive line charge," Brown wrote in his autobiography. "We worked at it as much as you groove a golf swing."

He believed that the most successful coach was not the one who invented the most plays but the one who adopted the best ideas of other coaches that fit his team in any given year. He introduced various shifting alignments that used decoying tactics so that enemy defenses never knew until the last second what formation Massillon planned to use. Because his players were so well-schooled, Brown's teams consistently defeated bigger, faster rivals. And by the time he left Massillon for Ohio State, his high school was scheduling opponents from as far away as New England to give his boys the best competition available.

Brown's success caught the eye of boosters at Ohio State, and, in 1941, the thirty-three-year-old coach became the youngest man ever to coach in the Big Ten. He introduced a system that combined the best elements of the single-wing and T-formation on offense, while sticking to the conservative 6–2–2–1 on defense. Seldom has a coach had such an immediate impact on a conference.

Ohio State lost but one game (to Northwestern behind the passing of Otto Graham) and tied one (against Michigan) in Brown's maiden season. In 1942, behind the running of nearsighted tailback Paul Sarringhaus and the signal calling of George Lynn, the Buckeyes astounded the nation by winning not only the Big Ten championship but also the national championship. The only loss in ten games was a 17–7 defeat to underdog Wisconsin. The Bucks' passing-oriented offense collected 337 points that season— the most in the Big Ten in twenty-six years.

Brown won with an ethical system that was second to none. He believed in all-out recruiting but despised teams that relied on under-the-table payments to win.

In addition, the coach insisted that his football players be excellent students, and he punished players who cut classes. Brown also mandated that his players keep in excellent condition, showing no tolerance for those who showed the least bit of flab on their bodies and insisting that they be "lean and hungry looking." The slender, balding coach fit this last description, too, so much so that sportswriter Red Smith once described Brown on the sidelines as "the homicide inspector viewing the body."

During the 1943 season, a poor year in which the coach had to make do with freshmen and scrubs because nearly his whole varsity had been drafted, Brown was part of one of the most unusual finishes to a college game in history. Essentially what happened is that after the coach led his team back to the dressing room following a game with Illinois that had ended in a 26–26 tie as an Ohio State drive stalled, an official entered the dressing room to inform Brown that a flag had been dropped on the final play of the game to signify an Illinois offside. Since a game cannot end on a penalty, Ohio State had the option of having one more play. With nothing to lose, Brown led his troops back onto the field to face Illinois. The few spectators that remained in the stands sat down to watch officials place the ball on the Illinois 28-yard line.

Brown ordered punter John Stungis to attempt a long

field goal. When the startled youth objected, saying he had never kicked a field goal, the coach reassured him: "There's nothing to it, John," said Brown. "I never missed a field goal in my life."

Stungis ran onto the field. The ball was hiked and set into position. Stungis got enough of his foot into the ball to send it over the upright with inches to spare, giving Ohio State a 29–26 victory. Later, the gleeful kicker asked Brown respectfully how many field goals had he kicked in his career. "None," Brown grinned. "I've never even tried one."

In 1944, World War II interrupted Paul Brown's career. He entered the navy as an officer and never returned to Ohio State. Instead, as the war wound down, he signed a five-year contract with Cleveland of the newly formed All-America Football Conference (AAFC) for what was then the biggest contract in the history of pro football: $25,000 a year and a share of the profits. After the appointment, his team was nicknamed the Browns in his honor, the first and only time such an honor has been given to a coach.

Those Cleveland teams of the late forties and early fifties boasted some of the finest players in the history of the game. Brown wanted no part of the color barrier that prevented black athletes from getting a shot at professional baseball and football; as a result, famed guard Bill Willis and such immortal running backs as Marion Motley and, later, Jim Brown, carved their names into the football record books at Cleveland.

Coach Brown convinced war veterans Lou Groza and Dante Lavelli from Ohio State to sign contracts with the Browns, as well as his old Northwestern nemesis, quarterback Otto Graham. But more importantly, he devised

Paul Brown

a workable system of recruiting players from all over the United States that put future stars such as Mac Speedie, a native of Utah, on Cleveland's roster. While other coaches chose their ballplayers from things they had read about them in slick magazines, Brown kept extensive files on every player he felt might be of use to him, the first scouting system. Like everything else the successful coach did, that system, too, was soon copied by the opposition.

Brown was offensive-minded and so left defensive preparations to capable assistants. From the moment the AAFC began, in 1946, Graham's powerful arm and Brown's brilliant mind revolutionized football's passing game. Formerly, there had customarily been one primary receiver on every passing play, while everyone else on the field either blocked or served as a decoy. Brown revolutionized the game not only by using primary and secondary receivers but also by requiring precisely run pass patterns that split enemy defenders. He also kept enemy defenses off balance by alternating his passing attack with trap plays, a fullback read-and-delay play, and a most effective quarterback draw in which Graham faked a retreat into the pocket before plowing straight ahead into whatever hole had opened up in the line. He even successfully employed the so-called "flea-flicker" play, where the quarterback hands off to a runner who, in turn, flips the ball back to the quarterback. This often drew in the secondary, allowing Graham to loft a bomb to a receiver all alone downfield.

One popular play that Brown rejected was the shotgun formation, in which a quarterback stands 6 or 7 yards behind the center to accept a direct snap. The reason he wouldn't use the play is that he feared that the snow and icy rain his teams were used to in Cleveland would hamper the quarterback's ability to catch the snap without fumbling. "Under those conditions, I doubt the shotgun would go off," he once quipped.

Brown insisted that all players on the roster memorize

what every other player on a given play was required to do. He eliminated guesswork and demanded precision on every play. Moreover, after 1950, when free substitution was allowed, the coach *called* nearly every play from the sideline as well, although he was wise enough to let Graham shout out audibles on the line of scrimmage if the enemy seemed to have guessed the play. Brown's usual method of sending in a play was to substitute his ends or guards, but on occasion the wily field general even sent in plays with an equipment manager, who ostensibly was in the huddle to check on some "damaged" equipment.

Brown's quarterbacks often complained about his so-called "messenger boy" system, but, according to sportswriter Jack Clary, the coach had one unrefutable answer. "If a quarterback wants to go home on Sunday night after we've played to watch films until midnight or 2 A.M.; if he wants to look at them almost every night of the week; and watch them in the movie rooms when we aren't practicing, then maybe he *should* call the plays."[1]

Brown also abolished such taboos as passing from your own end zone, confident that Graham could run or throw out of trouble. In fact, Brown's use of a big, rangy quarterback who was a threat to roam was another innovation copied by practically every professional team today. What was not always copied was how he treated his players like college boys, demanding that the team see movies en masse the night before a game and insisting that individual players develop clean living habits or be gone. He remained aloof from his players so that he could make objective decisions about their talents. For every player who loathed Brown's authoritarian ways, however, there were a dozen more who not only approved of his methods but copied them as well.

"The biggest influence on my coaching life has been Paul Brown," said Don Shula, a former Brown defensive back and one of more than a dozen head coaches who played or coached for the master. "Paul believed that everything stemmed from learning. He said that you learn by seeing, hearing, writing, practicing, and reviewing."[2]

Cleveland won the AAFC's first championship with a commendable 12–2 record, repeating three successive years until three AAFC teams merged with the NFL in 1950. Then, to show that his success in the so-called inferior league was no fluke, Brown took Cleveland to the NFL title game for six straight seasons.

Partly due to some successful lobbying against Paul Brown by a disgruntled Jim Brown—who had been called on the carpet several times for running afoul of the law—and partly due to the lack of support from the Cleveland owner, the head coach was ousted after the 1962 season. The owner added a final insult after dismissing Brown by ordering the coach's office cleaned out and the contents left on the fired employee's porch.

Brown reentered the pro game in 1966, when Cincinnati was added to the league as an expansion team to begin operation during the 1968 season. The new general manager/coach quickly showed that he had not lost his quiet toughness. Proving that he demanded nothing less than total obedience, he traded a veteran star who had the audacity to whisper during one of the coach's team meetings. He advised all "tramps, boozers, and barroom ladies' men" to change their ways or permanently change from their uniforms into civilian clothes. "If the game's worth something, it's worth everything," he told the Bengals. "I want you to give everything."

Brown quickly traded those players he perceived to be clubhouse lawyers, complainers, and malcontents. "A winner never whines," he once said.

Unfortunately, the Bengals faired poorly in the NFL player allocation draft, but Brown, as usual, selected wisely over the years in the college draft, most notably quarterback Ken Anderson. In both 1970 and 1973, Brown's Bengals finished first in the American Conference's Central Division. And in 1975, Brown led the Bengals to a wildcard playoff spot on the strength of an 11–3 record. But a players' strike and defections to the newly formed World Football League had disillusioned him. He stepped down as head coach but remained with the team as general manager. He saw the seeds that he had sown bear fruit in 1981, when Anderson quarterbacked the Bengals to a Super Bowl appearance, but the Bengals fell to the San Francisco 49ers 26–21 in Super Bowl XVI.

8

BOB DEVANEY: OVERCOMING A LATE START

Bob Devaney failed to earn his first head coaching position until he was forty-one, but he made the most of his opportunity when it finally came. During his career as a head coach, which lasted only from 1957 to 1972, he boasted a sensational .806 winning percentage. His teams at the University of Wyoming and the University of Nebraska won 136 games against only 30 losses and 7 ties.

This great coach came from humble origins—a working-class family. He was born in Saginaw, Michigan, on April 13, 1915, the son of Ben and Grace Devaney.

Unlike many top coaches who also starred as players in their youth, Devaney was a less-than-spectacular athlete who played at Alma College, a tiny Michigan school that was better known for producing academicians than athletes. In his first game as a player, Devaney had three teeth knocked out, and things didn't get any better for him after that. He liked to joke that although he majored in economics at Alma, he was a flop when it came to finances. The future coach—married as a sophomore to Phyllis A. Wiley—owed the school $350 upon his graduation, and he had to sweep floors and pump gas to pay off the debt before the registrar would release Devaney's diploma.[1]

Following graduation, Devaney coached football,

basketball, and baseball in addition to teaching six classes in high schools located in such isolated Michigan towns as Birmingham, Keego Harbor, and Alpena. "I worked sixty to seventy hours a week, which came out to about fifty cents an hour," recalled Devaney, "and I deserved every penny of it."[2]

After toiling fourteen years as a high school head coach, Devaney had amassed a respectable record, but he was an unknown outside of Michigan's boundaries. Finally, he was given an opportunity to become an assistant coach at Michigan State University under head coach Biggie Munn, and he stayed on after Duffy Daugherty replaced Munn. That offer, Devaney told John Underwood of *Sports Illustrated*, was "where my real life began."

The offer couldn't have come at a better time for the thirty-seven-year-old coach who admitted he was burnt out by all the hours required by his job. "If a break didn't come before I was forty, I was going to go back and get my Masters and take a boring administrative job somewhere," he admitted to Underwood.

In 1957, Devaney earned his first head coaching assignment when Daugherty recommended him for an opening at the University of Wyoming. After Devaney left Michigan State, Daugherty's record was never quite as impressive again, demonstrating the tremendous effect his assistant had upon Spartan players. Although Daugherty admitted to Wyoming officials that Devaney looked nothing like such glamorous coaches as John McKay and Bud Wilkinson, he said they'd never regret their choice. "Devaney is like an old shoe," said Daugherty. "You want to turn back to him after those stylish, narrow ones start pinching your feet."[3]

Devaney achieved immediate success at Wyoming, winning four Skyline Conference titles in five years. It was at Wyoming that Devaney picked up a reputation for being something of a character. On one occasion, Devaney told John Underwood, he and several players interceded when a native New Yorker on the roster got into a scrap with a policeman in a hotel lobby one evening. The policeman told Devaney that the player would have to stay in jail overnight. "If he stays, we all stay," Devaney shot back impetuously. The next thing the coach knew, both he and his players were spending the night on cots in the local jail.

On another occasion, reported *Sports Illustrated*, Devaney fell asleep in a university automobile after a banquet, rolling it down an incline. Thinking fast, the coach told his bosses that he had swerved to avoid a deer.

Devaney's philosophy was that football was a game best played loosely. For that reason, he once hired a magician to entertain his Wyoming players a couple of hours before a tough match against heavily favored Kansas. Apparently, the ruse worked. Devaney's Cowboys, 12-point underdogs, fought the Jayhawks to a 6–6 tie.

In 1962, Devaney left Wyoming for the challenge of a Big Eight coaching offer at Nebraska. Once again, his impact was immediate. His Cornhuskers won a postseason bid by impressing football experts with an unexpected 8–2 record. In the Gotham Bowl, his charges held on against Miami to return to Lincoln with a 36–34 victory.

Devaney, an unpretentious man, showed no signs of head-swelling after his Gotham Bowl win. To be sure, he did exchange his baggy serge suits for snappy red blazers with crimson hats to match, but even so, his clothes always looked as if he had jogged in them before he left for work that morning. He looked like a Russian peasant out on the town—all jowls and folds of fat—but a sharp mind was at work there.

To be sure, Devaney's teams were methodical and confident, reflecting the coach's own personality. Interestingly, the players dressed as sloppily on the field as their coach often did off it. Next to Penn State's drab uniforms, Nebraska's outfits and helmets were the least handsome in college football. Players frequently competed with socks rolled down around their ankles and their shirts torn or worn outside their pants. They may have looked ugly, but they did win.

Even though the coach's appearance was unprepossessing, Devaney was one of the college game's most determined coaches. Nebraska became a ball-control team, hanging onto the football for more than half the game while the clock wound down. Devaney's philosophy was simple but wise: "If your offense hangs onto the football," he reasoned, "the other team cannot score." In addition, he was a genius at spotting weaknesses in his opponents and making the most of them.

Coach Bob Devaney turned football into a respected sport in the state of Nebraska. Before he assumed the head coaching duties at the University of Nebraska, the Cornhuskers were considered college football's favorite patsies. In the twenty-one years prior to Devaney's appointment, the Huskers had enjoyed only four winning seasons, and in the six years prior to his coming, the team had won only nineteen of its sixty games.

In the team's history, Nebraska had only twice been ranked among the nation's top ten teams, and it hadn't won a Big Eight championship in more than two decades. Nebraska was regarded by coaches (such as ex-Huskers Fielding Yost and Dana X. Bible) as a steppingstone to more respectable positions elsewhere.

But Devaney brought his winning ways with him from the University of Wyoming to Nebraska, although he cloaked his seriousness behind a clownish mask. "I don't expect to win enough games to be put on NCAA probation," he joked upon his arrival. "I just want to win enough to warrant an investigation."[4]

Devaney succeeded beyond the most optimistic Husker fan's expectations, winning twenty-eight of his first thirty-three games. Much of the reason for his success was that he built a loyal staff at Wyoming that followed him to Nebraska. So much did he value their advice that when the University of Miami approached him about a head coaching job, Devaney turned it down flat because his assistants did not want to leave Lincoln.

During Devaney's eleven years in Lincoln, Nebraska, his teams dominated college football, winning 83 percent of their games and vying with Oklahoma year after year for Big Eight supremacy. The Cornhuskers probed enemy offenses and defenses for weaknesses, hammering away after they located them. At the same time, Nebraska's offense worked constantly to achieve the most favorable field position, while the team's defense concentrated on simply holding the line.

During the 1971 season, boasting one of the finest teams in college football history, Devaney saw success at both goals in certain important areas. Nebraska—which had been selected as the national champion in the Associated Press poll one year earlier, after knocking off Louisiana State University in the Orange Bowl 17–12—averaged an awesome 38 points a game in 1971, and the defense allowed but 6.4 points per game, tops in the country. After going 13–0, Bob Devaney's Huskers became the consensus national champion in 1971 in both the AP and UPI polls.

The highlight of that national championship season was the bitterly fought Nebraska-Oklahoma contest, which pitted two All-Americans, slotback Johnny Rodgers of Nebraska and running back Greg Pruitt of Oklahoma, against one another. Played on national television in Norman, Oklahoma, on Thanksgiving Day, the Cornhuskers-Sooners' clash is generally regarded as one of the finest all-time college games in history.

Nebraska started the scoring early in the game when Rodgers, destined to edge Pruitt for the Heisman Trophy

Bob Devaney

in 1972, ran back a punt 72 yards for a touchdown. Oklahoma quickly cut the margin by kicking a field goal, but Huskers' quarterback Jerry Tagge initiated a drive of 54 yards for a second touchdown, scoring on Jeff Kinney's 1-yard plunge. But Oklahoma courageously fought back, led by quarterback Jack Mildren from Green Bay, Wisconsin, who passed for one touchdown and ran 3 yards for another, going into the locker room at halftime with a 17–14 lead.

But the second half turned out to be Jeff Kinney's turn to show his skills. He scored three touchdowns on 154 yards rushing in the second half, helping Devaney's Huskers win a 35–31 thriller over Coach Chuck Fairbanks' Sooners.

Devaney always was a go-for-broke coach in the closing moments of a football game. "Go for touchdowns," he advised, "no field goals for ties." He didn't believe in fancy plays; no strange shifts or gimmicky plays for him. He showed you power and skill every time, daring you to outmatch him. "They'd come into your place and completely overwhelm you," Don James, now head coach at the University of Washington, once admitted while serving as an assistant at Colorado. "While I was at Colorado we never beat them. [We] had a tough time with Devaney's teams. It was like sending a bull terrier against a lion and saying, 'Sic 'em!' "[5]

Perhaps Colorado assistant athletic director Fred Casotti best described how opponents feared Devaney's Huskers, when he compared the Huskers with the Oklahoma Sooners. "It depends on how you want to die," said Casotti. "Oklahoma kills you quick, like a dagger in the heart. Nebraska slowly gives you cancer."[6]

At Nebraska, Devaney's strategy was to play his strength against his opponent's strength. He always managed to recruit gargantuan linemen—affectionately called "orangutangs" by the coach—who were as tough as steaks cut from range cattle. These linemen stalled even the most punishing running teams in the conference, giving them no yards and a cloud of dust. Envious coaches who charged that Devaney was recruiting immense blockheads who were academically deficient were quickly proved wrong; Nebraska demonstrated an impressive graduation rate of 75 percent of its players.

The heart of the University of Nebraska offensive line, under Devaney, was the offensive center. Nebraska normally assigned the best athlete among its linemen to the center position, where he was expected to show leadership and hustle while anchoring the line.

The Nebraska center was asked not only to block the man opposite him but on occasion to move swiftly to the left or right to cut down the left or right defensive guard. He needed to be strong and tall enough to protect the passer in the pocket but also swift enough to "do a do-dad" (push him out of the play in Nebraska parlance) on a linebacker when asked, as shown in the following diagram:[7]

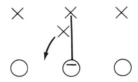

Offensively, during the 1971 national championship season, Devaney cleverly alternated the I-formation and the spread formation, taking advantage of I-back Jeff Kinney's powerful running in the first formation and Johnny Rodgers' elusive moves in the second. The spread formation, also known as the shotgun, allowed quarterback Jerry Tagge to stand 7 yards behind the center to take a direct snap. The spread formation was particularly effective during the last two minutes of a game in those rare situations where Nebraska needed some quick points for a win.

Incidentally, Devaney always believed that his players had to look at even a national championship in perspective. Consequently, before the start of the 1972 season, he originated a "Back to Earth Day" to remind his players that a tough season was ahead. Unlike many coaches who gained a swollen head after winning the national championship, Devaney remained a smalltown boy at heart. He was always doing small favors for the men and women everyone else ignored, including buying flowers on Mother's Day for all the women in the cafeteria who served players during training meals.

Devaney also differed from coaches such as Bear Bryant, who believed that all practices had to be brutal, punishing affairs for the players. Devaney never scrimmaged during the week, maintaining that his players absorbed enough bruises and bumps on game days. As a result, he seldom lost players due to practice-related injuries. However, lest his philosophy be mistaken for softness, the coach expected his men to demonstrate hardnosed, crushing physical play on the field every Saturday. Even so, he believed in platooning players at such demanding positions as quarterback and running back, thus keeping his players fresh for action in the crucial last minutes of a game.

Much of Devaney's success came from his personal charm and Irish gift of gab, making him the ideal recruiter. He quickly demonstrated that while he expected to recruit blue-chip hometown boys (believing that local boys play hardest in front of their families and friends), he had no qualms about going elsewhere to seek talent. In the spring of 1964, for example, no fewer than 68 of the 109 players who showed up at the first practice were out-of-state students. Although Lincoln is hardly a hub of urban activity, Devaney had considerable success attracting top players from such Midwestern cities as Chicago, Detroit, and Cleveland.

Devaney always had success recruiting the sons of Midwestern farmers. A smart man who took an interest in everything, even the price of pork bellies, he was never at a loss for words when traveling on recruiting missions around the state.

But if Devaney impressed the fathers, he was doubly effective around impressionable mothers. To recruit a West Virginia high school right end named Tony Jeter, who had all but promised to sign with Arizona State, the coach actually lent his tenor voice to a family hymnfest. "After that there was never a doubt in my mamma's mind where I was going to college," said Jeter. "I was going to play for that nice Mr. Devaney."[8]

But occasionally the last laugh was upon the coach, a self-deprecating man who loved to tell stories about himself. Another time that he joined a mother in song did not quite work to his advantage.

According to Devaney, he walked in upon a prospect's mother, who happened to be playing religious music at her organ at the time. Seizing his chance, the coach belted out a couple of hymns, immediately gaining her confidence. But his mission, the coach replied sadly, was all for nought. "The prospect enrolled at the University of Missouri," said the coach. "His mother, however, decided to go back to college. She, of course, enrolled at Nebraska."[9]

Such disappointments were rare, however. In his era at Nebraska, the hefty Devaney outcoached the likes of Bear Bryant, Ara Parseghian, Woody Hayes, and John McKay. And when he retired from coaching in 1973 (retaining his role of athletic director), the good work Devaney began was continued by his able successor, Tom Osborne, who, with Devaney, made Nebraska one of the most respected names in the history of college football.

9

BEAR BRYANT: NOTHING BUT A WINNER

Paul William (Bear) Bryant coached for thirteen years at the University of Kentucky, Texas A. & M. University, and the University of Maryland before returning to the University of Alabama, his alma mater, to coach for another quarter century. During his career, Bryant won 323 games, lost only 85, and tied 17, making him the winningest all-time coach until Grambling's Eddie Robinson surpassed him.

Robinson himself once acknowledged Bryant as a master of the game. "As long as they kick the ball off, there will always be some of Coach Bryant's philosophy in the game," said Robinson.

Few people have come from poorer circumstances than those in which Bryant grew up. Born on September 11, 1913, the next to last child of Wilson and Ida Bryant's family of twelve, young Paul grew up on an isolated Arkansas farm 5 miles from Kingsland. Even now, it takes better than two hours by car to drive north to Little Rock. The Bryants were poor, subsisting on the vegetables they grew and "poor man's bread"—baking powder, flour, and water covered by more flour and water for gravy.

As a boy, Paul earned fifty cents on a good day by breaking his back in a cotton field. Because his father was not a well man, and many of his siblings had grown and fled the family nest, Paul wound up responsible for the family's well-being while still in knickers. Such poverty proved to be an excellent, if grim, motivator later in his life.

Bryant learned early to put up or shut up. In the book *'Bama and the Bear* (1983), Bryant's friend W. R. Benton recalled the time that Paul bragged he could run six miles "in such-and-such a time." Friends pooh-poohed his boast, which angered him, and he wound up betting what little money he had that he could do what he claimed. "Well, he took off and we followed him in a car to make sure he didn't cheat any," said Benton. "By golly, he did it. It damn near killed him, though. He made it in the time he said he could run it."

Another dare accepted by young Bryant gave him something to remember for the rest of his life. When a traveling bear act came to the Lyric Theater in Fordyce, a town seven miles from the Bryant farm, some high school friends taunted Paul until he agreed to wrestle the bear for a dollar a minute. Young Bryant made a valiant attempt, but when the bear drew blood, he bolted into the front-row seats. "After the show was over I went around to get my money, but the man with the bear had flown the coop," wrote Bryant in his autobiography. "All I got out of the whole thing was a nickname."[1]

There was a saying in the South that hard work was for fools and mules, but young Paul's labors to help his family gave him the muscles of a man. Perhaps the most significant break in his life came when his mother rented a large house in Fordyce and turned it into a rooming house. Had he remained on the farm, his education might have ended with elementary school. At least it is unlikely he would have participated in sports. His father, who was sick and elderly, hated football, preferring that his children find what he considered gainful employment.

Given an opportunity to play sports at Fordyce High School, Bryant turned out to be a natural athlete, despite

his inexperience. The youth's strength and speed convinced the Fordyce coach, Bob Cowan, to play Bryant at offensive end and defensive tackle, and the boy was named All-State in his sophomore year. Although his grades were poor and he had a notorious reputation as a truant and fighter, Bryant used his football prowess to earn a scholarship to the college of his choice, the University of Alabama.

Soon after his arrival, Bryant admitted in his autobiography, he grew tired of school. He wrote his cousin, Collins Kilgore, to say he'd be leaving. "Go ahead and quit, just like everybody predicted you would," Kilgore wired back.[2] Needless to say, Bryant stayed. Fortunately for him, he met a campus beauty queen named Mary Harmon Black, who tamed the Arkansas roughneck. The couple married in 1935 after a short engagement and eventually had two children, Mae Martin and Paul, Jr.

Bryant played end for coach Frank Thomas' Crimson Tide teams. The 1934 national championship team won ten games without a loss in regular season play and trounced Stanford, 29–13, in the Rose Bowl played in January 1935.

Thomas, Bryant's college coach, had the look and voice of a drill instructor. Although only 5 feet-8 inches and 160 pounds, he had no compunction about tangling with one of his giant linemen if he was provoked. "I'll kick you right over the gymnasium," he shouted at massive tackle Bill Lee one day, while trying to crawl up the offender's chest.[3] A one-time star Notre Dame quarterback, Thomas showed players that his own college coach, the legendary Knute Rockne, had taught him well. Bryant later admitted that Thomas scared him to death, and this was one reason why the young end played several games during the 1935 season with a broken leg.

Paul "Bear" Bryant

Thomas advocated the single-wing system, a formation that relied on power plays and double-team blocking, which he used to overpower the opposition's weak side. According to sportswriter Edwin Pope, one of Thomas' more effective plays was the tailback-spin-to-feed-fullback. "As Alabama's tailback pivoted and handed off to the fullback, both guards pulled out of the line," wrote Pope. "The weak-side guard blocked the end. The strong-side guard took the linebacker."

Thomas could also win with razzle-dazzle. In his autobiography, co-written by John Underwood, Bryant recalled a curious "corkscrew play" off a punt formation. "The ball went to the left half who faked to the fullback and gave it to the tailback coming up the middle, with the quarterback and the guard trapping," wrote Bryant. "We beat Tennessee with it first time we used it, in Knoxville."

A typical Thomas team played steady, unspectacular football with considerable emphasis on defense. His teams were always well conditioned by his demanding practices—twice daily, once in full gear—under the baking Tuscaloosa sun, and Bryant was no less a drill sergeant when it came his turn to coach.

That turn came in 1937 when Thomas, advising Bryant to turn down three offers to play professional football, offered him an assistant's position. Three years later, Vanderbilt coach Red Sanders made him a better offer to become his first assistant coach, and Bryant moved to Tennessee.

After interrupting his career to serve in the U.S. Navy, attaining the rank of lieutenant commander, the thirty-two-year-old Bryant won his first head coaching position at the University of Maryland in 1945. From the start, he demonstrated his capacity for building a squad from scratch, using mainly older players—war veterans—to shape a defensive-minded team that went 6–2–1. Unfortunately, Maryland President H. C. (Curly) Byrd, who had coached Terrapin teams for twenty-three years before becoming an administrator, undercut his new coach's authority. The president dismissed an assistant coach of Bryant's and reinstated a player—the son of a politician—that the Bear had dropped from the squad. In a story that made headlines in the nation's sport sections, Bryant resigned, a move that caused a student strike at Maryland.

Head coaching jobs at Kentucky (1946–1953) and Texas A. & M. (1954–1957) followed. Bryant's finest season in Lexington was his 11–1 record in 1950, including an upset of top-ranked Oklahoma in the Sugar Bowl. With the Aggies, Bryant overcame a disastrous 1–9 freshman year to compile three successful seasons.

By the time he and his 91–39–8 record arrived back at the University of Alabama in 1958, Bryant had a well-earned reputation as a taskmaster. He was so demanding, players liked to kid, that even his shadow called him "sir." One year, at A. & M., he started with a squad of a hundred players; ten days later, only twenty-nine players were left, as a result of his Bad News Bear's version of boot camp. "They say I teach brutal football, but the only thing brutal about football is losing," said Bear, responding to his critics. "If it's worth playing, it's worth paying the price to win."

No one worked harder than Bryant himself, whose capacity for putting in long hours was best expressed when a reporter, tongue-in-cheek, asked the coach if it were true he could walk on water. "If I do," Bryant quipped, "I do it before most people get up in the morning."

Bryant, like other great coaches, built his reputation by developing defensive teams that gave up scores the way a miser gives up hundred-dollar bills. His philosophy was simple but unarguable: If the other team can't score, it can't win. What he could not tolerate were what he called "easy" touchdowns: scores made on a long bomb, the 99-yard kickoff return, the breakaway run. He also worked to eliminate silly mistakes on defense and offense as well—the missed signals, penalties, and bonehead decisions that take the heart out of a team. He convinced his teams that there was no excuse for the opposition to score just because it stood only 3 yards from the end zone. In one season alone, Alabama stopped teams cold inside the 3-yard line nineteen times.

The head coach used imagery to motivate his defensive players, asking them to pretend they formed a fence surrounding the football. He advocated the theory that the best defense was also an offensive weapon, maintaining his whole life that theoretically there are more ways for the defense to score than there are for the offense to do so.

Bryant believed strongly that statistics told how good or bad his defense performed. He wanted defensive backs to intercept one pass out of every thirteen thrown, and he wanted the defense to force three fumbles per game, recovering at least two. Alabama's defenses traditionally felled enemy ball carriers during the course of a game, because Bryant stressed gang tackling.

Curiously, Bryant did not so much innovate new strategies as perfect old ones. He was the consummate pack rat, always on the phone in contact with other coaches, staying abreast of tactical developments in the game. At Kentucky in 1950, for example, he borrowed Georgia Tech coach Bobby Dodd's playbook and consulted with Oklahoma's Bud Wilkinson to perfect a split-T formation to benefit his then-hot young quarterback, Babe Parilli, destined for eventual glory in the NFL and AFL.

"Coach Bryant wasn't the greatest when it came to Xs and Os," revealed Bear's longtime assistant, Sam Bailey. "But he was a genius at managing people and getting the most out of people."

Bryant believed in changing his system to fit his personnel, not the other way around. His adaptability certainly contributed to his success in the college game for so many years. Another indication of his worth as a coach was the number of former Bryant assistants and/or players who wound up in coaching themselves, including his successor, Ray Perkins, now coach of the Tampa Bay Buccaneers; Pat Dye of Auburn; Danny Ford of Clemson; Steve Sloan, former Duke coach and present University of Alabama athletic director; and Jackie Sherrill of Texas A. & M.

One offensive play that was essentially all Bryant's own was a play that worked so well for years that it seemed almost illegal. The rules committee finally did outlaw it.

Another brainstorm that came to him one night in a dream before the 1950 Sugar Bowl was to play four tackles on defense against the University of Oklahoma. By "playing the corners up tight," said Bryant, the defense gave Kentucky the equivalent of a nine-man line in a 13–7 win over Coach Bud Wilkinson's top-ranked Sooners. He used two tackles in place of one end and a middle guard, erecting a veritable stone wall in front of Oklahoma's split-T offensive front line.[4]

Bryant was also bright enough to realize the importance of game films. At Texas A. & M., during his disastrous freshman season (when the Aggies went 1–9), he won his only game against a strong, tough Georgia team, because he and his assistants used films to spot flaws in Wally Butts' Bulldogs. After the Georgia quarterback called a running play, he lined up his feet parallel to the line. When the signal caller wanted a pass, he unconsciously shifted his rear foot in the direction he planned to throw. With that much information, Bryant's Aggies slipped past Georgia 6–0, averting a winless season.

After four years in College Station, Bryant's Aggies won the Southwest Conference championship in 1956 and a Gator Bowl bid in 1957, prompting the now-sorry University of Alabama to make him an attractive offer in 1958 to save a program that had soured. The Crimson Tide had lost twenty-eight of its last thirty-six games.

Immediately after his arrival back home in Tuscaloosa, the new coach started motivating his men. He hung up a sign that read, "Winning isn't everything, but it beats anything that comes in second." He also started the 100

Percent Club; only players who gave their all could join. Bryant's record at Alabama made him a national legend. When he retired in 1982, after thirty-eight years as a head coach, Bryant's 323 wins were the most victories by a coach in major college competition. Most impressive, under him Alabama won national championships in 1961, 1964, 1965, 1973, 1978, and 1979.

The homespun Bryant liked to say that his entire philosophy of football stemmed from a day he spent watching ants build an anthill while he was stationed in Africa during the war. In his book, *Bear Bryant on Winning Football* (1983), Bryant said he was impressed with the way ants worked in many small groups to complete the large project. "There was no inactivity, no wasted motion," he wrote. "There was unity and there was a plan." Consequently, ever since, Bryant broke his team into squads, trying to keep all his players busy in the spirit "of teamwork and cooperation."

At Alabama, one strategy that Bryant stressed more than most coaches was the importance of his special teams, particularly in the kicking game. The Crimson Tide drilled constantly on kickoff and punt coverage, as well as on the protection of field-goal kickers. He insisted that teams well schooled in the kicking game were also, by necessity, always in tip-top condition.

Bryant also strove to recruit top-notch quarterbacks, as evidenced by the likes of Joe Namath, Ken Stabler, and Richard Todd—all of whom went on to impressive professional careers after leaving Alabama. He frequently said that the quarterback had the single most important job on a football team. Bryant regarded the selection of plays as the position's most important task, and he allowed quarterbacks to call all plays unless they proved unfit. In that case, he and his coaching staff took over from the bench, because poor play selection destroyed a team's morale quicker than any other factor.

In the book *Bear Bryant on Winning Football,* the

coach said he broke every football field into seven parts. The first was from his own goal line to the 3-yard line, which he called the Must Zone, because the team needed to advance the ball far enough to give the punter at least 13 yards of room to kick the ball downfield from the end zone. The Third-Down Zone went from the 3-yard line to the 25-yard line. Bryant wanted his quarterback to call trap (short for mousetrap) plays in which an offensive lineman abandons his position to block a defensive lineman who has intentionally been allowed into the backfield. The First Down Zone extended from the 25-yard line to the 40-yard line, and was so called because Bryant said it was essential to gain 10 yards in order to enter the Free-Wheeling Zone.

The Free-Wheeling Zone extended from Alabama's 40-yard line to the opponent's 40-yard line. Bryant felt that the offense had a big advantage here, and that intelligent play selection in this zone could really confuse the defense. The Scoring Zone extended from the 40-yard line to the 200. Here Bryant recommended the use of trick plays and plays designed to yield quick scores.

Bryant believed that it was harder to score from the Gut Zone, which extended from the 20-yard line to the 4-yard line. He recommended that teams pass on first down to gain a minimum of 5 yards, noting that it was important to outgut the defense. The Self-Scoring Zone included the 4 yards in front of the other team's goal. He advocated that the ball here should only be carried by the best ball carrier or the quarterback himself to reduce the possibility of a fumble.

Bryant stayed in the game until December 15, 1982, retiring with an uncharacteristic 8–4 season his final year. On January 26, 1983, just six weeks after his retirement, he died of a massive heart attack.

The news shocked the nation. Bear Bryant's numerous successes had lulled people into thinking the poor boy from Arkansas was immortal.

10

JOE PATERNO: HIS DEFENSE NEVER RESTS

Head coach Joe Paterno is a rarity in his profession—he has devoted his entire life to working at a single college. After thirty-seven years with Pennsylvania State University's Nittany Lions, the last twenty-one as head coach, the sixty-year-old Paterno is regarded as the unofficial patriarch of college football. He has turned down offers to coach pro football (from Pittsburgh and New England) that would have made him a millionaire, because he feels it is more important to work with young people than to make money.

But Paterno is not famous merely for his longevity and loyalty to one institution. He is regarded as one of the brightest minds in the game. His innovations, particularly in the area of defense, are imitated by many coaches on levels from junior high to the pros. For Joe Paterno, it's been every which way but lose. His record as head coach includes 199 wins, 44 losses and 2 ties for an .816 winning percentage. The Nittany Lions under Paterno have ranked in the hotly contested national "Top Ten" no fewer than fifteen times since he became a head coach. Over the years his teams accomplished thirty-one, twenty-three, nineteen, and fifteen consecutive game winning streaks, and they have played in eighteen postseason bowl games. In 1987, Penn State won a coveted national championship by thwarting Vinny Testaverde and his University of Miami Hurricanes 14–10 in the Fiesta Bowl, made sweeter when *Sports Illustrated* named Paterno its Sportsman of the Year. In 1982, his 11–1 Lions also earned the nation's top ranking by defeating the University of Georgia's Bulldogs 27–23.

Paterno says he is equally proud of his team's graduation rate, consistently one of the highest in college football. He encourages his players to study as hard as they play, and he considers himself an educator. For many years, he has been a gadfly in the sides of other coaches, urging that they put their athletes' educations before football in importance.

"I don't want to pat myself on the back, but I never wanted to be just a football coach," says Paterno, who even *looks* like a professor with his eyeglasses and conservative suits. "It's important that the faculty understand that I think football has a place in the university, and that the tail's not wagging the dog."[1]

As testimony to the effectiveness of his philosophy, nearly 90 percent of the coach's players earn diplomas, compared to some so-called major football factories where as few as 14 percent graduate. He brags more about today's dentists, architects, and even a Nashville songwriter who played ball for him than he does about his many great football players who went on to star in the pros.

Paterno was a scrawny but determined youth. He was born December 21, 1926, the son of an Italian-American high school dropout who bettered himself by attending college at night for decades. Joe and his brother George starred in football for Brooklyn Prep and were nicknamed "The Gold Dust Twins" for their considerable talents. During the offseason, he recalls, "I used to be an usher at Ebbets Field," for the Brooklyn Dodgers.

Following high school graduation, Paterno attended Brown University to study English literature. There he quarterbacked for two winning teams (7–2 in 1948 and

8–1 in 1949) and impressed Charles A. "Rip" Engle, his coach, with his fine mind. "He can't run and he can't pass," a sportswriter back then said of him. "All he can do is think and win."

After earning his degree, Paterno's career took an unexpected twist. He had planned to attend law school, but when Engle accepted the head slot at Penn State, he invited Paterno to coach the offensive backs. Quickly the young assistant developed a reputation as a coaching genius. Several colleges tried to woo him away, but he rejected all offers, preferring to wait for Engle's inevitable retirement.

For thirty-seven years Paterno has lived in the shadow of Pennsylvania's Nittany Mountains. Married to a Penn State graduate named Suzanne Pohland, he is father to five children. He admits that his job forces him to spend twice the time that a normal person spends working, taking him away from his family. Much of that time is spent deep in concentration in his study, doodling out new plays, formations, and concepts. He takes a cerebral approach to football.

Paterno, who draws up his strategies at home while listening to opera music, is a changed person when he straps on cleats. Biting humor and angry tirades are his manner of attack, although many say he has mellowed slightly with age. He resembles a terrier, snapping at the heels of breeds far bigger than he, to keep them hopping. But although Paterno drives his players mercilessly, he knows the wisdom of easing up when he senses that they are overworked.

Paterno recruits players who share his drive and intelligence, but he knows better than to carry a bag of tricks that is too heavy for one team. He claims that there is

Joe Paterno

such a thing as preparing too many plays for a game. Therefore, before every game, his coaches not only introduce new plays but cancel some pet plays, too. Paterno insists that strategies be introduced or canceled on the Tuesday of game week. Early in his career, he found that changing strategies the Thursday or Friday before a game gave his team insufficient time to become comfortable with changes and led to misplays.

After narrowly defeating Kansas State University in a 17–14 away game back in 1969, the coach revealed his basic defensive philosophy to reporters. "Football games are won or lost on five or six plays," he said. "The trouble is you never know when they're coming."[2]

Because of that belief, Paterno trains his defense not to *look* for big plays but to expect them to occur, and to make the most of them when they do. Early in his career, the coach's critics accused him of being "lucky," because his team won so many games on recovered fumbles, blocked punts or kicks, and interceptions. But after the Nittany Lions won year-in and year-out by capitalizing upon enemy mistakes, it became apparent that Paterno's strategy centered on letting his opponents beat themselves. His teams are well schooled in the art of forcing turnovers.

For his offensive and defensive players alike, Paterno offers several pet theories that he recites over and over. His players often seem amused or irritated that he uses them so often, but they cannot deny that such stratagems work. Perhaps the coach's most important maxim is that his team always play as if it were winning even when they are behind. Paterno rarely puts emotion into talks with his team, but when the Lions come into the locker room on the short end of the score, he urges his team to play as loose and aggressively as if they were ahead. Like his hero, General George Patton, Paterno believes that those who think they are destined for great things *do* great things. He communicates this belief to his players to motivate them. "Let me know how good you want to be," Paterno tells players on the first day of practice. "If you want to be national champions, I'll show you how to be national champions."

Perhaps because Paterno doesn't believe that winning is the only thing in life, he isn't afraid to lose a game. A tie, however, sticks in his throat like a fishbone. This is why his teams have tied only two games in two decades. Given a choice of tying a game with an easy one-point kick or going for a difficult two on a run or pass, Paterno chooses the latter every time, and holds his head high when he loses. "A man's reach must exceed his grasp," Paterno tells his players, stealing advice from the poet Robert Browning, "or what's a heaven for?"

In 1973, Coach Paterno was asked to deliver a commencement speech to a Penn State graduating class. What he said to them revealed something significant about his coaching philosophy. "Don't look for touchdowns all the time," he counseled. "Think about hitting in there tough, play after play, and then the big play will present itself."

Paterno urges his players—particularly members of the defensive secondary—to be rambunctious and take calculated gambles. "Always go for broke," he tells them again and again. *The Sporting News* once said that Paterno coaches football the way the brash, aggressive Jackie Robinson used to play baseball. By gambling intelligently and striving to block kicks, pick off enemy passes, and sack quarterbacks, Penn State manages to win more than its share of those six or seven "big plays" in a game that Paterno feels ultimately lead to victory. He never rebukes a player who follows a gut instinct, even if that man disobeys a coaching order.

Paterno considers his defense to be an extension of the offense. If his defense scores a safety or winds up in the end zone on an intercepted pass, the points on the board count just as surely as if his own offense had earned them.

University of Akron head coach Gerry Faust sums

up Penn State's defensive formation like this: "Penn State employs basically an eight-man front on defense, with four downline men, four linebackers, and a three-man zone secondary. From this basic front, they do a lot of shifting and sliding, trying to create confusion." Joe Paterno calls this restless defense a 4-4-3, and it has become one of the most imitated defenses in football. With the help of assistants from the NFL's Chicago Bears and Denver Broncos, the coach has adapted the system to the demands of the pro-set offenses his opponents such as Alabama throw at him. His opponents often label it a "stacked" defense because the linebackers are aligned right behind the four front linemen.

The beauty of Paterno's defensive formation is that it changes shape in amoeba-like fashion. The coach calls it his "magic defense," because of its "Now you see it, now you don't" possibilities. Given the down, game situation for the offense, and score at the time, Paterno has the choice of shifting the linemen and linebackers, so that as many as *eight* men can settle on the line. This, as you can imagine, is a frightening sight for the five men on the offensive line. They frequently become rattled and blow either the snap count or their assignments.

Having a hard-rushing defense has many advantages for Penn State. They frequently manage to get through to the quarterback for a sack or allow only very brief yardage should the quarterback elect to run. In one season (1969), for example, Penn State's defense held all quarterbacks in ten regular season games to minus 11 yards.

The defense also thwarts teams that rely on an inside power running game. Those running backs that the charging front four rushers cannot stop, they at least manage to slow down, for the linebackers to knock down. By way of example, during the 1970 Orange Bowl, Penn State kept Missouri running back Joe Moore to a scant 36-yard total gain after he had rushed for 1,300 yards in ten regular season games. In the 1983 Sugar Bowl, less spectacularly, the Lions held Georgia's Heisman Trophy winner Herschel Walker to 103 yards in twenty-eight carries in a contest that Walker was expected to dominate. This was Walker's second-lowest total since his freshman year.

Paterno's strategy to stop the powerful backs is a simple one. The defense is instructed to seal all cracks that would enable the likes of a Walker to get up a head of steam in the open field. Another rule is that the front four try to make the runner run east-west, or across the field, not north-south, or up and down the field, to prevent him from making those long gainers that spell points on the scoreboard. When a truly powerful runner has the ball, Penn State defenders are ordered to tackle him from the waist down. Shoulder tackles are too easily broken.

But Paterno never frets about the total yards his opponent gains. He worries about the bottom line: How many points has the other team scored? During the 1987 national championship game, the Lions won despite gaining only 162 yards to Miami's 445. One of his pet sayings is that his defense must learn to be like the willow. "Bend but don't break," he says.

Intense pressure on the quarterback from the line is naturally appreciated by Paterno's pass defenders. Forced to either release the ball too soon or swallow it whole, many quarterbacks elect to attempt dangerous passes into heavy downfield traffic. To illustrate this effectiveness, consider that Penn State holds the Orange Bowl record for interceptions, with seven in one game (1970). Another game plan Paterno used to win the 1987 championship was to allow Miami's receivers to catch the ball but force turnovers with bone-crushing tackles.

In a nutshell, Coach Paterno's defensive players take advantage of the rule that allows the defense—unlike the offense—to move about before the snap. Before Paterno became so successful, many coaches relied on defenses that were as "set" as offensive formations. As a result of his ingenuity, defensive players not only became more mobile, but offensive players were forced to guess what the defense might throw at them next. A major advantage of such strategy is that Paterno's teams wear down enemy offenses. By hammering them for the first three quarters, Penn State wins many games against exhausted teams in the fourth quarter.

Paterno, for many years, was a member of the old coaching school that said when you throw the ball, two of the three things that can happen are bad. In other words, if you don't catch the pass, it will go as incomplete or into the arms of a defender.

"Interceptions drive me nuts," Paterno told a reporter for the *New York Times*. "I'm not a reactionary—I just want to win a couple of football games."

Thanks to the national championship he won after the 1983 Sugar Bowl, in great part due to the strong throwing arm of Todd Blackledge, Paterno in recent years has allowed his Lions to rely more on the passing game. Under no circumstances, however, will a Paterno offense ever become as pass-oriented as, say, Brigham Young University's. He allows his quarterbacks to throw up to twenty-five times in a game, less than half as many passes as BYU attempts in a given game.

Paterno's outspoken manner and innovative mind have stamped him as one of college football's truly great coaches. He admits that both Rip Engle, his old coach, and Vince Lombardi, "a guy who came from the same neighborhood in Brooklyn that I'm from," were important early influences upon him. But mainly, says Paterno, he is responsible for his own successes and few failures.

"All of us who become a success in coaching have got to have some kind of competitive instinct," he says. "I knew I could never be a Rip Engle and never be a Vince Lombardi or a Bud Wilkinson. I really tried hard to be myself, figuring that kids could smell a phony. I don't think you can fool them."

TOM LANDRY:
THE BEST BLACKBOARD
COACH IN FOOTBALL

Until Tom Landry was born, on September 11, 1924, the most famous man to claim tiny Mission, Texas, as his birthplace was the star of many B Westerns, Ken Maynard. One of four children born to the town's volunteer fire chief, Ray Landry, and his wife, Ruth, Thomas Wade Landry excelled both in academics and sports at Mission High School. Not only was he named to the National Honor Society, but he was also named to the All-South regional team in football. This combination of brains and football savvy has helped Landry become one of the most successful professional coaches in the modern era. Going into the 1987 season, Landry—the only coach the Dallas Cowboys have ever had—had a 260–157–6 record to show for his twenty-seven-year career.

Landry's excellence can be seen by looking at his overall coaching record. The Cowboys under Landry have the National Football League's second-best record (Miami's is best) since 1970, the year the NFL and the AFL merged. The Cowboys are tied with the Dolphins for most Super Bowl appearances (five) and have appeared in ten conference championship games—the best record in pro football. Dallas also holds the record since 1970 for most playoff seasons, with fourteen.

As a boy, Tom was devoted to his father. His life nearly ended at age three, in fact, when he ran out into the street to welcome his father back from a hunting trip, suffering a broken leg when a car broadsided him.

But young Landry prospered under his father's attention. Later, under the guidance of an understanding high school coach named Bob Martin, he found that his calling was in football. Landry was already a disciplined young man, but even if he were not, he would have kept curfew around his coach, because Martin was his next-door neighbor and could see for himself how late the boy stayed out. In Landry's junior year, the young quarterback threw several touchdown passes and scored 46 points himself to help his team win its district championship. In his senior year, the thin six-footer switched to tailback as Mission ran the Notre Dame box formation, leading his team to a 12–0 season and outscoring the opposition 322–0. But because Tom was so modest, his parents had to read about his exploits in the newspaper, even when he made one of his frequent runs for 50-plus yards. He refused to tell anyone much more than the score of the game, fearing that someone might think him a braggart.

From Martin, Landry learned the value of teamwork. His coach's motto was "Eleven brothers are hard to beat."

Martin believed that Landry won more games with his heart and head than he did with raw talent. "Tommy wasn't fast, but he was smart," Coach Martin revealed in *The Man Inside Landry* (1981), a biography of the coach that was written by Bob St. John. "He knew how to run, giving them the limp leg, picking his way."

As a result of his heroics, Tom was recruited by all the right Texas schools, but he chose the University of Texas, partially because he felt it was close enough to Mission that his parents might get to see him play. But after an outstanding 1942 season with the freshman team, Landry was assigned to military duty with the Eighth Air Force. He served as a B-17 co-pilot and fought in thirty combat missions above war-raked Europe. Landry had a personal vendetta against the enemy. His brother Robert, Tom's elder by three years, perished when his air force plane burst into flames on a routine mission over Iceland.

As a co-pilot, Landry helped his crew out of danger on more than one occasion by keeping calm while others panicked. Once, when all the engines had conked out on his plane during a bombing run over Germany, the pilot and other crew members prepared to bail out, but Landry stayed at his station and fiddled with the controls to alter the fuel mixture, managing to restart the engines. Had the crew parachuted into enemy territory behind the lines, there is little doubt Landry and the others would have spent the duration of the war in a POW camp.

Typically, Landry refused to divulge any details about his heroic actions during the war. "Oh, we got a few holes in our bomber every once in a while, but nothing much happened, really,"[1] Landry told a curious sportswriter in Bob St. John's presence.

Following the war, twenty-three-year-old Tom Landry, then a wiry 190-pounder, returned to the University of Texas. His wartime experiences made him seem much more mature than many of his younger teammates. Because his hair had begun to thin already, he even looked more like a coach than he did a player.

Landry's first varsity coach in 1946 was Dana Xenophon Bible, a well-known football fundamentalist who was coaching his thirty-third season and who would retire that year. Bible, whose record was 205–73–20, believed in no-frills football, relying mainly on the single-wing attack. Both Bible and his successor, Blair Cherry, felt that quarterback Bobby Layne was the best man for the quarterback job, relegating Landry to a backup position on offense, as well as full-time duties as a defensive back and punter. But against North Carolina, when Landry was given an opportunity to play fullback, he ran for 91 yards on twelve carries. In his junior season, he was named second-string fullback on the All-Southwest Conference team, and the following year, he was named co-captain of the Longhorns.

Landry's finest game was his last as a senior. In the Orange Bowl against heavily favored Georgia, Landry played both fullback and defensive halfback, gaining 117 yards on only seventeen carries, as Texas defeated the Bulldogs, 41–28. As he walked off the field, Landry was intercepted by an assistant coach of the New York Yankees of the All-American Football Conference (AAFC) and offered a $7,500 contract. A few weeks later, in January 1949, Landry married a lovely blonde-haired sophomore named Alicia Wiggs and buckled down to finish his last semester's work toward his B.A. degree from Texas.

Landry lasted but one year, 1949, with the Yankees, because the next year the AAFC consolidated with the NFL, and he wound up playing across town for the New York Giants. The merger profoundly affected Landry's future, as he ended up playing ball as a defensive back under the coach of the Giants, Steve Owen, also known as the "Father of Defense," who coached from 1931 to 1953.

Owen respected Landry, who even jumped in to play two games as quarterback when New York's two quarterbacks were injured. The Texan quickly proved a student of the game, compensating for a lack of speed by reading defenses as well as anyone in the league and by memorizing the routes of receivers to cut down their advantage. He was the first player to develop what came to be known as "keys" to what the enemy offense had planned, concentrating hard to spot tendencies that teams seemed to have in given situations. Almost singlehandedly, Landry, while still a player, used knowledge of the opposition as a defensive weapon.

"We didn't have words like 'keying' in those days," Landry's fellow defensive back, Emlen Tunnell, told Gary Cartwright, a *Sport* magazine writer. "Tom made up his own keys and taught them to the rest of us."[2]

In those days, defensive formations were pretty much the same old tired 5–2–4 or 5–3–3 against passing teams, or 6–2–3 against predominantly ground-gaining clubs. But against Paul Brown's powerful Cleveland Browns, Owen conceived the idea of an "umbrella defense"—so called because it opened up like the spokes of an umbrella—which packed six men on the line and four men deep in back, leaving but one linebacker to roam freely all over the field. But better able to construct a play than explain it, Owen pressed Landry into service to diagram the play for his teammates on a blackboard. It was as a result of that experience that Landry thought that he, too, could coach professional football.

Incidentally, the 6–4–1 defense managed to stop the running of powerful Marion Motley and the passing of all-time great Otto Graham. Landry's Giants defeated the Browns 6–0, handing Paul Brown the first shutout of his career. And later that season, Owen and Landry repositioned the umbrella slightly, taking one man off the line and throwing a fifth man deep to help the Giants eke out a 17–13 win against the Browns in a rematch.

When Owen retired, the Texan became even more valuable as a defensive strategist to head coach Jim Lee Howell. Howell named Landry a player-coach, lauding him as "the best coach" in pro football. This was heady praise indeed, considering that Howell's offensive coordinator was a young genius named Vince Lombardi. The two assistant coaches made a curious team; Lombardi was fire, Landry was ice.

Landry's major break came in 1960. The National Football League expanded, and Dallas hired him as head coach with a ten-year contract. His first years were rough. The Cowboys lost every game that first year and, by 1965, had only a so-so .500 record under the new head coach. But what the head coach had done was to plan a long-range attack, developing young players who would be with him for the long haul, not buying decaying veterans simply to win two or three games.

119]

Before too long, both sportswriters and his players were calling him one of professional football's best strategists. In one *Sport* magazine interview, former Dallas defensive back Charlie Waters called Landry "the best blackboard coach" he'd ever seen.

"I used to love those Wednesday meetings when he'd give us our game plan—the precision, the neatness," raved Waters. "I mean, some coaches you can't even understand what they're writing up there. Landry is not only neat, his game plans are always real smart analyses of the other team's weaknesses."[3]

Moreover, Landry developed not only outstanding players but also turned his assistants into men who made fine head coaches. Although Landry's assistants are so loyal to him that he has had only twenty-four assistants in twenty-seven years, seven of those men (Gene Stallings, Dick Nolan, Dan Reeves, Mike Ditka, Sid Gillman, John Mackovic, and Raymond Berry) went on to head their own teams.

These coaches couldn't have found a better man to emulate than Landry. Always dressed in a tie and dress hat, almost always poised and in control of his emotions no matter what the score, Landry wears the mask of a sphinx on the field. Because he is conscious of playing a role, he purposely keeps his distance from his men. "Secretly, I guess, I'd love to get close to my players," Landry admitted to writer Jack Clary, author of *The Gamemakers*. "But you're never able to do things you really love to do. Some of the greatest guys I know are football players, and I'd like to be part of things with them because I have such a great feeling for them. But it's still impossible to break down that barrier. . . . It's an injustice to the player to get too close to him. Subconsciously, he'll tend to use that as a crutch."

Tom Landry

Tony Dorsett, a great Cowboy running back since 1977, is one player who has chafed under Landry's aloofness. But even he accepts Landry's methods, although grudgingly. "I've been here a long time, and I can't say I know the man," Dorsett told *Sport* magazine. "Every other system I have been in I have known the coach. But this is a business. That is Landry's philosophy of doing things. I have always tried to put myself in his shoes. I figure he doesn't get close to his players because it would make it tougher than it already is to cut a player."[4]

But despite his coolness, Landry underneath is a warm man who can even crack a joke on occasion. Congratulated by reporters after his announcement in 1981 that he would return for yet another season, Landry quipped, "One way to look at it is that I haven't had a promotion in twenty-one years."

Landry spends much time with his players on fundamentals, examining game films and his own ideology. Although he sometimes appears frustrated because his players do not possess his ability to understand football concepts almost intuitively, he goes over details again and again until he is certain he's gotten through to them. Landry's offense, like that of San Francisco 49ers coach Bill Walsh, relies on multiple formations to confuse enemy defenses. Frequently, the Cowboys like to line up before the snap and move to two or even three formations before the final count. Landry loves plays involving subterfuge, particularly plays that make suckers out of the defensive ends while his running back goes roaring up the sideline like a fast train. His offense is designed to let defensive men take themselves out of a play just long enough to let an elusive back such as Tony Dorsett through the slimmest holes.

His defenses are equally complex. He employs both man-to-man and zone coverage, giving Dallas as many as seven different ways to protect against the pass. In the early seventies, blessed with his "Doomsday defense," he relied on 4–3 coverage (using two linemen in a so-called Flex arrangement to halt trap plays). In more recent years, however, adjustments against today's passing game became necessary. Landry now blitzes frequently, but for years he used to send in only one man on a blitz. An important facet of Landry's defense is that a defensive player must remain glued to his area of turf no matter which way the play flows. Players must control the urge to abandon their positions when it looks as if the ball carrier is headed to the opposite side of the field.

"You've got to have a clear-cut philosophy to be successful, and it must be transmitted to your players," Landry told Jack Clary. "They must thoroughly understand everything you are trying to do, so much so that eventually it simply becomes instinctive to them. I don't say that my philosophy is the only one. It is the only one for me and the right one for my team. There are many successful philosophies because there are many successful coaches. . . .We want everyone on the same path, to know where we are going and what our goals are."[5]

More important than merely setting goals, says Landry, is discovering the best way to achieve those goals, and then sticking with the plan—even through lean times—until success is achieved. Although the coach surrounds himself with the latest in computer software and other technological advances, he maintains that football games are won or lost by human beings. He believes that the success of the Dallas organization comes down to his own insistence on having quality players, coaches, scouts, and a team image.

And, no question, Dallas has become a symbol of football superiority—"America's Team"—as its many fans call it. The list of quality players who starred for Landry is a long one: quarterbacks Don Meredith, Roger Staubach, and Danny White; tight end Mike Ditka; receivers Drew Pearson, Lance Alworth, and Bob Hayes; running backs Duane Thomas, Tony Dorsett, and Herschel Walker;

and defensive specialists Lee Roy Jordan, Cornell Green, Herb Adderley, Mel Renfro, Bob Lilly, Jethro Pugh, Randy White, and Ed "Too Tall" Jones.

Landry's list of great years is equally long. Dallas captured Eastern Division titles in 1966 and 1967. Then, in 1971 and 1972, the Cowboys went to the Super Bowl, losing the first to Baltimore, 16–13 but winning the second against Don Shula's Miami Dolphins, 24–3, behind the strong passing arm of Roger Staubach. In 1976 and 1979, the Cowboys lost Super Bowls X and XIII to Pittsburgh, 21–17 and 35–31, respectively. Dallas, however, managed to trounce Denver, 27–10, in Super Bowl XII.

In recent years, however, Landry's magic formula has lost some of its potency. The 1986 season, in particular, devastated Landry and his millions of followers. The Cowboys, for the first time since 1965, failed to produce a winning record, thus ending a streak of twenty NFL seasons with a record of .500 or better. Dallas fans were talking Super Bowl after the Cowboys, led by Herschel Walker (who played four positions), reeled off six victories in eight games. But the rest of the year proved dismal, and the season ended with a 7–9 record.

There was some talk that Landry might retire after the 1987 season, but the coach himself denied it. "I could hardly leave the team in the shape they're in right now," he told sportswriter Jim Dent.

Chances are, however, that the famed coach's demise, in the words of Mark Twain, has been greatly exaggerated. As Landry enters his twenty-eighth season, Dallas fans bet that the Cowboys can turn misfortune around to give the coach one more Super Bowl appearance before he hangs up his hat forever.

12

DON SHULA: THE MAN WHO LIVES TO COACH

The only NFL head coach to coach in a Super Bowl before reaching his fortieth birthday, Don (Shoes) Shula is regarded as one of the most emotional men in the game. He has become the winningest active coach in football, not only by his mastery of football Xs and Os but also by displaying a powerful will to win. "Don Shula is competitive in everything," his former assistant coach, Monte Clark, once told the *New York Times*. "He's competitive eating breakfast."

Don Shula is a throwback to the great Vince Lombardi. His twice- and thrice-daily practices during a six-week training camp under a blazing midsummer Miami sun are frequently compared to the rigorous sessions that the Green Bay Packers conducted during their championship seasons under head coach Vince Lombardi. Shula, now fifty-seven, is said by his former players to have softened some. But don't expect current members of the Miami Dolphins to agree. His booming voice is said to leave scorch marks on the uniforms of his players when he is angry, and his belief in rigorous conditioning is every bit as strong as it was when he began his coaching career a quarter century ago. "If you win, it makes for an easier life," admitted Shula's former all-star running back, Larry Csonka, "because if you lose, Shula goes crazy."

Shula displayed a competitive spirit even as a youngster. He was born January 4, 1930, in Grand River, Ohio—
now a suburb of Cleveland but then a pretty village—one
of six children of Dan and Mary Sule. His father—a Hun-
garian immigrant who worked as a fisherman on Lake Erie
for $100 per month—changed his name to Shula to make
it easier for Americans to pronounce. Young Donald Francis
Shula was a poor loser who once hid beneath the grand-
stand to cry when his elementary school football team blew
its championship game. When eight-year-old Don lost a
meaningless game of cards with his grandmother, he ripped
up the deck—the wrong thing to do in the authoritarian
Shula household.

The elder Shulas did not approve of Don's manic
obsession with sports, and they particularly worried when
he came home from football practice at Harvey High School
with a bloody gash across his nose. His mother and father
refused to let him play again, but he went against their
wishes by forging a parents' permission slip to attend practices. After his parents finally learned what he had done,
they attended a game in which Don returned a punt 75
yards and became his biggest fans.

Raised a staunch Roman Catholic, Shula attended
the Jesuit-run John Carroll University in Cleveland on a
football scholarship. Hampered by injuries much of his
career, Shula's best season was in 1950, when the halfback
gained 1,080 total yards rushing and receiving as his Blue
Streaks won eight games and lost only two. His unheralded
club defeated powerful Syracuse 21–16 in a game scouted
by the Cleveland Browns, and Shula battered his way to
gain 125 yards rushing. A few months later, the Browns'
legendary coach, Paul Brown, drafted the son of a poor
fisherman in the ninth round. The chances looked slim to
none of Shula making the talent-rich Browns, but the
young man turned down a tempting opportunity to coach
a high school team, reasoning that he might be selling
himself short.

"I knew that the coaching job would be gone, but I felt that there would be others," Shula wrote in his autobiography (co-written by Lou Sahadi), *The Winning Edge* (1973). "Right then I formed a philosophy in life that has remained with me. I always want to do the best that I can with the opportunities that God has given me. The only way that you can do that is to give yourself the chance to go as high as you possibly can. If you don't have the confidence in yourself and you don't have the desire to compete and move ahead, then you start to get stagnant. . . . If I fall a little bit short, then I'm still further ahead than if I hadn't reached at all."

During training camp, Shula found himself quickly ahead of all other rookies. The best thing about playing for John Carroll was that Blue Streaks' coach Herb Eisele ran a pro style offense and defense patterned after those used by the Cleveland Browns. So well did Shula understand the system that he managed to become the only rookie kept by Brown during the 1951 season and was paid $5,000 for it. Used exclusively as a defensive back, Shula made the most of his opportunity when veteran Tommy James was hurt, intercepting six passes.

Unfortunately, his career with the Browns ended prematurely in 1953. Shula revealed in *The Winning Edge* that one day he opened his newspaper to the sports section only to read that Cleveland had traded him to Baltimore. That would be the first time he would play in front of fans other than from his hometown.

The trade proved wonderful training for a future coach. In addition to playing cornerback for the Colts, Shula served as the defense's field general, calling signals. In the first half of the season, he gained his reputation as a defensive expert. His calls resulted in so many interceptions and recovered enemy fumbles that Baltimore's defense became known as the Radar Corps.

His last year as a player was in 1957, when he played with the Washington Redskins. By 1960, after brief coach-

127]

ing stints as an assistant at the Universities of Virginia and Kentucky, Shula rejoined the pro ranks as a defensive backfield coach with the Detroit Lions. He also married a girl from his hometown named Dorothy Bartish in July 1958, proposing to her (and receiving her acceptance) by mail.

Shula's opportunity to become a head coach happened years before he thought it would come. Thanks to a demolishing of the Green Bay Packers in a nationally televised Thanksgiving Day game, the young defensive coach gained an instant reputation as a defensive wizard. Consequently, when Detroit played Baltimore near the end of the 1962 season, Colts' owner Carroll Rosenbloom approached him.

Shula later recalled that conversation in his autobiography.

"Are you ready to become a head coach?" asked Rosenbloom, hardly the sort to mince words.

"The only way that you'll ever be able to find out is to hire me and let me show you that I am capable of being a winner," Shula replied.[1]

A few weeks later, Rosenbloom took a chance, hiring Shula to guide the fortunes of the 1963 Colts. Only thirty-three, he was younger than some of his players, and he had played at Baltimore with such veterans as Joe Campanella, Bill Pellington, and Gino Marchetti. Nonetheless, the new coach quickly asserted his authority, challenged only by Johnny Unitas, the temperamental future Hall-of-Fame quarterback, who occasionally snapped at his boss during the heat of a game.

First and foremost, Shula considered himself a teacher. His experiences as an assistant at Virginia and Kentucky had taught him that not all players grasped information

Don Shula

as quickly as he once did in college. He also learned that you cannot stress fundamentals too much or too often, and that even All-Pro veterans required refresher courses in proper techniques before bad habits became ingrained. His chalk sessions resembled a college classroom. He and his assistants passed out new plays on mimeograph paper, and they encouraged players to underline important bits of information. "In football, it's not what you know but what your players know that counts," he told a *Washington Post* reporter.

The worst thing a player can utter after making a mistake in front of Shula is the excuse, "I thought you said. . . ." The effect is like waving a bloody steak in front of a tiger. He can devastate players who fail to concentrate. He rarely drafts players who do poorly on tests, believing that raw talent without intelligence is not enough to win. As a result, his teams lose few games because of mental errors, and they consistently draw the fewest number of penalties in the NFL. Shula never lets an error escape unchallenged, always drilling for precision in every practice. "Uncorrected errors will multiply," he once said. "Someone once asked me if there wasn't benefit in overlooking one small flaw. I asked him, 'What is a small flaw?' "

But Shula's Midwestern frankness and friendliness have always showed players that he cared for them as individuals. He seems to possess a teacher's innate knowledge of which players need a scolding, which players need policing, and which players need buckets of praise. The only fault he has demonstrated is that of a terrible temper in times of defeat. His powerful lungs have forced more than one hulking player to cower in the clubhouse following a loss.

An admitted workaholic, Shula has always put in from fifteen to eighteen hours a day on the field, insisting upon living at a dormitory with his players from the first day of practice until the last day of the season. Nonetheless, even though seeing his family only twice a week, his marriage has thrived. "I'm fairly confident that if I died tomorrow, Don would find a way to preserve me until the season was over and he had time for a nice funeral," his wife Dorothy once said tongue-in-cheek.

Shula's marriage to the Colts, however, turned rocky after seven successful years. After an unspectacular first season, Baltimore went 12–2 in 1964, only to lose to the Cleveland Browns 27–0 in the championship game. He had other great years in Baltimore, such as the 1967 club, which finished at 11–1–2. The 1968 team went to the 1969 Super Bowl on the strength of a 34–0 shellacking of Cleveland in the championship game. Unfortunately, Joe Namath and the New York Jets of the upstart American Football League upset the heavily favored Colts, 16–7, in a game that destroyed owner Carroll Rosenbloom's faith in Shula. The coach remained one more season and then accepted a similar job with Miami, then the joke of the NFL.

Since joining the league, the Dolphins had won only fifteen of fifty-six games, and their 1969 record showed only three wins. "I'm no miracle worker and don't make me out to be one," he told reporters at his first press conference. "I don't have a magic formula. I'm not a person with a great deal of finesse. I don't have peace of mind until I know I've given the game everything I can, because the whole idea is somehow to get an edge. . . . I try to [get an edge] with mental preparation, and physical preparation. . . . You set a goal to be the best and then work hard every hour, every day, to reach the goal. If you allow yourself to settle for anything less than being number one, then you're cheating yourself."

Another time, Shula summarized his belief in the Puritan ethic for reporters. "I'm just a guy who rolls up his sleeves and goes to work."

Joe Robbie, the Miami owner, wanted instant results, Shula recalled in *The Winning Edge*. When a fan asked

Robbie how long the new man had to turn the program around, the owner snapped, "He's got all summer." Surprisingly, that was all the time Shula needed to succeed.

In 1970, Shula won coach of the year honors for the third time. His well-conditioned Dolphins surprised the NFL by finishing with a 10–4 season—good enough to make the playoffs, though Miami lost a disappointing game to Oakland in the first round of post-season play. But Shula's men came back to appear in three straight Super Bowls, losing to Dallas in 1972 but winning Super Bowl VII against Washington, 14–7, in 1973 and Super Bowl VIII against Minnesota, 24–7 in 1974. The victory in Super Bowl VII gave Shula's 1972 squad a perfect 17–0 record— the only team in NFL history to go undefeated for an entire season.

After his arrival in Miami, Shula won with an incredibly uncomplicated ball-control offense, operating from two set formations. (Many NFL teams used more than a hundred sets.) Shula's first formation, dubbed the "Brown," had quarterback Bob Griese call play-option passes. In this lineup, the fullback, Larry Csonka, lined up directly behind the quarterback. Griese's favorite play in this set was the Quick-I, where he faked to one of his powerful backs, Mercury Morris, Jim Kiick, or Csonka, to paralyze the linebackers and cornerbacks; then he threw to his great receiver, Paul Warfield, on a slant-in pattern. This play was so popular with then-President Richard Nixon that he called Shula at 1:30 in the morning to suggest that the coach use that play in the 1972 Super Bowl against Dallas.

To compensate for a less-than-perfect offensive line, Shula ordered Griese to abandon the pocket by dropping straight back, dodging the first rusher to gain penetration and rolling. If Griese elected to hand off, he called a steamrolling, inside running play, with Kiick or Csonka carrying the ball and the remaining man acting as a blocking back.

Shula's second formation, the "Red," had both the fullback and halfback split wide of the quarterback to employ end sweeps and short, dump-off passes or crosses to tight end Marv Fleming. Split end Paul Warfield, in the Red formation, lined up next to the offensive tackle on the weak side. Depending on the call, Warfield either crossed with Fleming or delayed a count to take a quick pop over the middle from Griese. Most of the time, Griese's secondary receiver was Howard Twilley, a slow-footed but sure-handed receiver who knew how to get open on one-on-one coverage through clever use of fakes and by running disciplined pass routes.

Perhaps because Shula as a player was a success more as a result of his determination than his ability, the coach always has taken a special pride in the accomplishments of overachievers such as Twilley. On the other hand, he trades or cuts all players who show less than 100 percent desire, labeling them "coach killers" because a coach often is fired before these players finally decide to play up to potential. Shula wants only players who have what he calls "the Winning Edge"—edge being an acronym for *e*xtra study, *d*etermination, "*g*assers" (being in top condition), and *e*ffort.

As might be expected of a former defensive back, Shula's defense during those early Miami years relied heavily upon young cornerbacks who were both quick to react and intelligent. Part of Shula's game plan every week was to determine what enemy receiver usually caught the ball in big play situations. Aided by impeccable scouting reports, the Dolphins consistently frustrated enemy offenses by stepping in front of opposing receivers to take the big plays away.

The cornerstone of the Miami defense was middle linebacker Nick Buoniconti, a small (5-11, 220-pound) overachiever who knew instinctively when to hold his position to stop the run and when to blitz into the enemy's backfield. "Letdowns are for losers," was Buoniconti's battlecry.

Shula's defense became known as the 5–3 defense, a rather confusing appellation that came to be called that because a key man in its success was number 53, Bob Matheson. Matheson, who played both defensive end and linebacker, alternated between two- and three-point stances. Sometimes he'd rush the passer; other times he'd drop back to aid the linebackers, leaving just three men to rush. The innovation, more often than not, rattled enemy quarterbacks and confused offensive lines. This defense was popularly known as the "No Name" defense, since virtually every starter was, like Buoniconti, an NFL retread or an unheralded unknown out of college.

Shula's fourth season with the Dolphins was another memorable year, as Miami continued to win until Oakland stopped their victory streak at nineteen. In the 1974 Super Bowl against Minnesota, the Dolphins collected but one penalty and suffered no turnovers en route to a 24–7 humbling of the Vikings.

As Shula has gained more experience, his plays have become more complicated, and he frequently draws upon the thousands of formations he's observed during his many years in the game. He demands that players be able to execute any offensive set in a given situation, deviating frequently from his game plan when an opponent's defense shows unexpected tendencies. He is not afraid to try something new in pressure-packed situations. During the 1985 Super Bowl against San Francisco, for example, he used a no-huddle offense during the first drive of the game to generate a score.

Shula's ability to change with the times accounts for his fantastic record. The Dolphins have only missed the playoffs five times under Shula, and his career 263 victories are second only to George Halas' 325 wins for the Bears. Only fifty-seven now, Shula seems a shoe-in to shatter Halas' record before he retires.

However, Shula's Miami teams in recent years bear little resemblance to the crushing, run-oriented offenses of those great Dolphin teams in the early seventies. Blessed with the talented arm of quarterback Dan Marino, but cursed with a running game that somehow had stalled, Shula tried unsuccessfully in 1984 and 1985 to win with a wide-open air attack.

But the Dolphins in 1986 were a more balanced team. And as they moved into Joe Robbie's spanking new stadium, Shula was determined to find a way to overcome weaknesses in the offensive line that have hampered the Dolphins' attack. "My Number One priority is I want to get this football team back on its feet where it belongs, up on the top," he told reporters on the day he signed a contract for his eighteenth season with Miami.

NOTES

Chapter One

1. Ellis Lucia, *Mr. Football: Amos Alonzo Stagg* (South Brunswick and New York: A. S. Barnes and Company, 1970), 56–57.
2. *College Football and All American Review* edited by Christy Walsh (Culver City, CA: Murray & Gee, Inc., 1949), 923. See also Lucia, *Mr. Football*, 85.
3. Lucia, *Mr. Football*, 95.
4. Formation taken from *Football*, by Amos Alonzo Stagg and H. L. Williams, published in 1893. This play was reprinted by John Durant and Les Etter, *Highlights of College Football* (New York: Hastings House, 1970), 84.
5. Paul Zimmerman, *The New Thinking Man's Guide to Pro Football* (New York: Simon and Schuster, 1984), 220.

Chapter Two

1. Edwin Pope, *Football's Greatest Coaches* (Atlanta: Tupper and Love, Inc., 1955), 121.
2. Clyde Bolton, *War Eagle: A Story of Auburn Football* (Huntsville, Alabama: The Strode Publishers, 1973), p. 71.
3. Pope, 126.
4. Johnny Martin, *Death Valley: 72 Years of Exciting Football at Clemson University* (Anderson, South Carolina: Independent Publishing Company, 1968), 183.
5. Martin, 185.

Chapter Three

1. Kenneth L. (Tug) Wilson and Jerry Brondfield, *The Big Ten* (Englewood Cliffs, New Jersey: Prentice-Hall, Inc., 1967), 133.
2. Pope, *Football's Greatest Coaches*, 315.

Chapter Four

1. Michael R. Steele, *Knute Rockne: A Bio-Bibliography* (Westport, Connecticut: Greenwood Press, 1983), 10.
2. Jerry Brondfield, *Rockne: The Coach, The Man, The Legend* (New York: Random House, 1976), 73–74.
3. Brondfield, *Rockne*, 83–84.
4. Pope, *Football's Greatest Coaches*, 197.

Chapter Five

1. Pope, *Football's Greatest Coaches*, 29.
2. Francis Wallace, "Gridiron Galahad," *Collier's* (October 14, 1950), 36.
3. George Lynn Cross, *Presidents Can't Punt: The OU Football Tradition* (Norman, Oklahoma: University of Oklahoma Press, 1977), 54–55.
4. John D. McCallum, *Big Eight Football* (New York: Charles Scribner's Sons, 1979), 3.

Chapter Six

1. *Lombardi: Winning Is the Only Thing*, edited by Jerry Kramer (New York: Pocket Books, 1970), ix.
2. Gene Schoor, *Football's Greatest Coach, Vince Lombardi* (New York: Pocket Books, 1975), 15.
3. Schoor, 58.

Chapter Seven

1. Jack Clary, *The Gamemakers* (Chicago: Follett Publishing Company, 1976), 39.
2. Don Shula with Lou Sahadi, *The Winning Edge* (New York: E. P. Dutton & Co., Inc., 1973), 81.

Chapter Eight

1. John Underwood, "And This Man Is at the Top," *Sports Illustrated* (September 13, 1971), 53.
2. McCallum, *Big Eight Football*, 198.
3. "Organization Man," *Newsweek* (October 4, 1965), 60.
4. "Rhymes with Uncanny," *Time* (November 19, 1965), 78.
5. McCallum, *Big Eight Football*, 179.
6. McCallum, *Big Eight Football*, 10.
7. *Football Coaching*, compiled by The American Football Coaches Association and edited by Dick Herbert (New York: Charles Scribner's Sons, 1981), 130.
8. "Rhymes with Uncanny," *Time*, 78–80.
9. McCallum, *Big Eight Football*, 199. Also, see Underwood, *Sports Illustrated*, 54.

Chapter Nine

1. Paul W. Bryant and John Underwood, *Bear: The Hard Life and Good Times of Alabama's Coach Bryant* (Boston: Little, Brown and Company, 1974), 27.
2. Bryant and Underwood, *Bear*, 43.
3. Pope, *Football's Greatest Coaches*, 269.
4. Bryant and Underwood, *Bear*, 102–103.

Chapter Ten

1. This quotation and all others in this section (unless otherwise acknowledged) are taken from Hank Nuwer's interview with Joe Paterno ("Joe Paterno: Thinking, Winning and Lasting") which appeared in the December 1985 issue of *Inside Sports*, 18–22.
2. Ridge Riley, *Road to Number One: A Personal Chronicle of Penn State Football* (Garden City, New York: Doubleday & Company, Inc., 1977), 443.

Chapter Eleven

1. Bob St. John, *The Man Inside . . . Landry* (New York: Avon Books, 1981), 46. Also published in 1979 by Word, Incorporated.
2. Gary Cartwright, "Tom Landry: God, Family and Football," published in *The Best of Sport: 1946–1971*, edited by Al Silverman (New York: The Viking Press, 1971), 468.
3. Joe Klein, "The Last Roundup?" *Sport* (December 1984), 48–50.
4. Gary Myers, "Tony Dorsett," *Sport* (December 1985), 17.
5. Jack Clary, *The Gamemakers* (Chicago: Follett Publishing Company), 104–105.

Chapter Twelve

1. Shula with Sahadi, *The Winning Edge*, 85–86.

BIBLIOGRAPHY

Blair, Sam. *Dallas Cowboys: Pro or Con?* Garden City, New York: Doubleday & Company, 1970.

Bolton, Clyde. *War Eagle.* Huntsville, Alabama: The Strode Publishers, 1979.

Brondfield, Jerome. *Woody Hayes and the 100-Yard War.* New York: Berkley, 1975.

Brondfield, Jerry. *Rockne: The Coach, The Man, The Legend.* New York: Random House, 1976.

Brown, Paul, with Jack Clary. *PB: The Paul Brown Story.* New York: Atheneum, 1979.

Bryant, Paul ("Bear") with a revision by Gene Stallings. *Bear Bryant on Winning Football.* Englewood Cliffs, New Jersey: Prentice-Hall, Inc., 1983.

Bryant, Paul W. and John Underwood. *Bear: The Hard Life and Good Times of Alabama's Coach Bryant.* Boston: Little, Brown and Company, 1974.

Cassady, Steve. *Super Bowl: Pro Football's Greatest Games.* New York: Scholastic Book Services, 1980.

Clary, Jack. *The Gamemakers.* Chicago: Follett Publishing Company, 1976.

Cohane, Tim. *The Yale Football Story.* New York: G. P. Putnam's Sons, 1951.

Cross, George Lynn. *Presidents Can't Punt: The OU Football Tradition.* Norman, Oklahoma: University of Oklahoma Press, 1977.

Dowling, Tom. *Coach: A Season with Lombardi.* New York: Popular Library, 1970.

Durant, John and Les Etter. *Highlights of College Football.* New York: Hastings House, 1970.

Ford, Tommy. *Bama Under Bear.* Huntsville, Alabama: The Strode Publishers, 1983 (revised edition).

Furlong, William Barry. "Coach with Winning Ways." *The New York Times Magazine.* (November 9, 1958): 26 + .

Herbert, Dick, ed. *Football Coaching.* New York: Charles Scribner's Sons, 1981.

Hyman, Mervin D., and Gordon S. White, Jr. *Joe Paterno: "Football My Way."* New York: The Macmillan Company, 1971.

Klein, Joe. "The Last Roundup." *Sport.* (December 1984): 46 + .

Kramer, Jerry, ed. *Lombardi: Winning Is the Only Thing.* New York: Pocket Books, 1971.

Logue, Mickey, and Jack Simms. *Auburn: A Pictorial History of the Loveliest Village.* Norfolk, Virginia: The Donning Company, 1981.

Lombardi, Vince, with W. C. Heinz. *Run to Daylight.* New York: Grosset & Dunlap, Inc., 1963.

Lucia, Ellis. *Mr. Football: Amos Alonzo Stagg.* South Brunswick and New York: A. S. Barnes and Company, 1970.

McCallum, John D. *Big Eight Football.* New York: Charles Scribner's Sons, 1979.

——————. *Southeastern Conference Football.* New York: Charles Scribner's Sons, 1980.

Martin, Johnny. *Death Valley: 72 Years of Exciting Football at Clemson University.* Anderson, South Carolina: Independent Publishing Company, 1968.

Micheson, Herb, and Dave Newhouse. *Rose Bowl Football Since 1902.* New York: Stein and Day, 1977.

Myers, Gary. "Tony Dorsett." *Sport.* (December 1985): 15 + .

Nuwer, Hank. "Joe Paterno: Thinking, Winning and Lasting." *Inside Sports.* (December 1985): 18–22.

Pope, Edwin. *Football's Greatest Coaches.* Atlanta: Tupper and Love, 1955.

Riley, Ridge. *Road to Number One.* Garden City, New York: Doubleday & Company, Inc., 1977.

St. John, Bob. *The Man Inside . . . Landry.* New York: Avon Books, 1981.

Schoor, Gene. *Football's Greatest Coach.* New York: Pocket Books, 1975.

Shula, Don, with Lou Sahadi. *The Winning Edge.* New York: E. P. Dutton & Co., Inc., 1973.

Silverman, Al, ed. *The Best of Sport: 1946–1971.* New York: The Viking Press, 1971.

Smith, Red. *To Absent Friends.* New York: New American Library, 1983.

Smith, Robert. *1964–65 Great Teams of Pro Football.* New York: Dell, 1964.

——————. *Illustrated History of Pro Football.* New York: Madison Square Press, 1972.

Staubach, Roger, with Sam Blair and Bob St. John. *Staubach: First Down, Lifetime to Go.* New York: Avon Books, 1976.

Steele, Michael R. *Knute Rockne: A Bio-Bibliography.* Westport, Connecticut: Greenwood Press, 1983.

"Super Bowl Scouting Reports." *Life* (January 14, 1972): 32–39.

Taylor, Curtis. *'Bama and the Bear.* Salt Lake City: Great American Sports Inc., 1983.

Underwood, John. "And This Man Is at the Top." *Sports Illustrated.* (September 13, 1971): 52 + .

Unsigned. "Organization Man." *Newsweek.* (October 4, 1965): 60.

Unsigned. "Rhymes with Uncanny." *Time.* (November 19, 1965): 78 + .

Wallace, Francis. "Gridiron Galahad." *Collier's.* (October 14, 1950): 36–40.

Whittingham, Richard. *Saturday Afternoon.* New York: Workman Publishing, 1985.

Wilson, Kenneth L. (Tug) and Jerry Brondfield. *The Big Ten.* Englewood Cliffs, New Jersey: Prentice-Hall, 1967.

INDEX